SOMERSET MONASTERIES

SOMERSET MONASTERIES

ROBERT DUNNING

TEMPUS

First published 2001

PUBLISHED IN THE UNITED KINGDOM BY:

Tempus Publishing Ltd
The Mill, Brimscombe Port
Stroud, Gloucestershire GL5 2QG
www.tempus-publishing.com

PUBLISHED IN THE UNITED STATES OF AMERICA BY:

Tempus Publishing Inc.
2 Cumberland Street
Charleston, SC 29401
1-888-313-2665
www.arcadiapublishing.com

Tempus books are available in France and Germany
from the following addresses:

Tempus Publishing Group   Tempus Publishing Group
21 Avenue de la République   Gustav-Adolf-Straße 3
37300 Joué-lès-Tours   99084 Erfurt
FRANCE   GERMANY

British Library Cataloguing in Publication Data.
A catalogue record for this book is available from the British Library.

ISBN 0 7524 1941 2

Typesetting and origination by Tempus Publishing.
PRINTED AND BOUND IN GREAT BRITAIN

Contents

List of illustrations

Text figures

Colour plates

Preface

At any one time during the Middle Ages members of religious orders were a very small proportion of the population, but their influence was far greater than their numbers would seem to have warranted. For the secular world religious men and women were a potent spiritual force, praying day and night for the salvation of souls; and as owners of extensive property monasteries were, collectively, and some like Glastonbury individually, an economic force of great significance. Some monks and nuns were known far beyond the confines of their cells and cloisters; most were not even known by name beyond their neighbourhoods and communities. By the nature of their confined lives they did not, as a rule, work together on a common programme nor speak with a more distinctive voice than the Church as a whole. Yet they were, of course, conscious of each other; partners in a great enterprise, travellers on the same road.

To choose to study the regular religious life of a single county is principally a matter of personal piety, a study I have been engaged on for nearly 40 years. Yet Somerset was virtually conterminous with the diocese of Bath and Wells, a structure within which most religious orders were happy to operate. Not all orders were represented, and just beyond its boundary were, for instance, the great houses for women at Shaftesbury, Wilton and Lacock which might well have drawn Somerset ladies from their native shire. Within it, however, was Glastonbury, whose distinction and, more important, whose surviving records, allow a balanced story of one county's religious life to be told.

I am grateful to two scholars of monasticism for reading my text and making comments which I have eagerly incorporated. Dr Sally Thompson quite rightly said I had not given enough attention to Somerset nunneries and I have tried to do justice to her pioneer work. Dr Joe Bettey as always gave generously of his time and expertise, pointing out omissions and suggesting improvements.

Acknowledgements

This book is the result of many years of learning from others as well as of studying sites and reading manuscripts. Among those who contributed were Mick Aston, Joe Bettey, Ian Burrow and Michael McGarvie. People who have given particular help are my colleague Mary Siraut, whose research into Stogursey and Yenston priories and into the records of some of Glastonbury's estate has been invaluable. David Bromwich finds the obscurest of printed sources with the greatest possible speed, and the help of Tom Mayberry of the Somerset Archive and Record Service has been equally valuable.

For use of illustrations grateful acknowledgement is made to the following: *Archaeological Journal* lxxxvii (1930), 443 for **29**; the Bodleian Library, University of Oxford, for jacket source and **colour plate 1** (MS Auct F 4 32, f.12), and for **41** (MS Bodl 80, f. 1v) and **42** (MS Hatton 30, f.73v); Cornwall Record Office for **19** (AR 27/10); the late James Stevens Cox for **54**; J.P.S. Dunning for **45** and **53**; English Heritage for **colour plate 3** (taken by author) and **34**; the Dean and Chapter of Exeter Cathedral for **60** (MS 800); R. Colt Hoare, *Monastic Remains of the Religious Houses at Witham, Bruton and Stavordale* (1824) for **8**, **9** and **12**; Lmabeth Palace Library for **35** (MS 99 f. 192v); the Lord Petre and Devon County Record Office for **48** (123M/01); *Proceedings of Somerset Archaeological and Natural History Society* for **4** (vol. xxiv, frontispiece), **14** (vol. viii, opp.80), **25** (vol. x, opp.89) and **32** (vol cxxxiv.146, plan by Ian Burrow); Public Record Office for **24** (C 258/28), **57** (SC 12/14/38) and **59** (LR 2/62); Somerset Archaeological and Natural History Society for **colour plates 22** and **29**, and **5** and **7**; Somerset Record Office for **15** and **17** (D/D/B reg 12 ff. 63, 97), **20** (D/B/bw 108), **22** (D/D/B reg 8, f. 197a), **26** (D/D/B reg 9, f. 119), **27** (D/D/Ca 10a, f.12), **49** (DD/L P32/26), and **55** (DD/GS 28); Charles Stopford Sackville and the Northamptonshire Record Office for **28** (SS 1980); the Dean and Chapter of Wells for **2** (MS Bk 7), **11** (ADO/9), **39** (MS Bk 7), and **43** (A.H. 103); the Dean and Chapter of Westminster for **33** (MS 16040).

The rest of the illustrations are from my own collection, some few deriving from that of Somerset County Council's Archaeology Department (the work of Mick Aston (**52**) and Bob Winn among others), others from the collections of the late W.J. Wedlake and Peter Greening (including the coloured aerial view of Woodspring priory (**colour plate 30**) by Jim Hancock).

Introduction

Somerset has a fair claim to importance in the history of the monastic movement. The travelling Welsh pilgrim saints like Decuman, Carantoc and Dyfrig who came to its western shores were preachers whose restless agenda did not include much quiet, communal contemplation, but the Irishmen who practised that kind of discipline had found the marshy remoteness of Glastonbury much to their taste, and the Irish influence on the life of St Aldhelm inspired him to found religious communities in the east of the county nearest his native Wiltshire at the end of the seventh century of which Bruton and Frome were among the most prominent.

Bruton and Frome became two among several religious centres which were soon to play a political role within the emerging kingdom of Wessex. As the Saxons moved westwards, an important part of their conquest was the conversion of the native peoples to their own, relatively newly-adopted, Christianity. Over the next three centuries or so perhaps as many as 20 minster churches were established in what later came to be Somerset, all of them probably with the support of the kings of Wessex, which were, in effect, bases of mission into the surrounding countryside. To Bruton and Frome, already established, were soon to be added Milborne Port, Doulting, Keynsham, Bedminster and Wells; and further south and west Yeovil, South Petherton and Crewkerne, North Petherton and Taunton. Wells was to have a special role from the year 909 when it became the seat of the Somerset bishopric. It was the first of the minsters to change its role.

Dunstan, a Somerset man by birth, played a vital part in the revival of monastic life based on the Rule of St Benedict, which was successor in western Britain to the Irish communities of the Celtic world. Dunstan's revival spread far beyond the confines of his native county in the tenth century, and the active and generous support of successive members of the Saxon royal house made Glastonbury one of the richest monastic foundations by the time of the Norman Conquest. Athelney, Bath and Muchelney, also founded with royal support, were necessarily paler imitations.

Reformed and often stricter versions of the monastic life as practised by those inspired by the continental communities at Cluny, Citeaux and later at La Grande Chartreuse offered the new landowners with estates on both sides of the English Channel the opportunity to be generous for the good of their immortal souls. The founder of a monastic house could expect considerable credit and respect in his lifetime, burial within the monastic precinct and the comfort of prayers for himself and his kin for ever. Smaller gifts of land or even sale at a reasonable price might provide similar benefits for lesser men. Montacute, Cleeve, Witham and Hinton were among the results of the generosity of the new landowners in Somerset, the first three during the great wave of monastic enthusiasm before the end of the twelfth century.

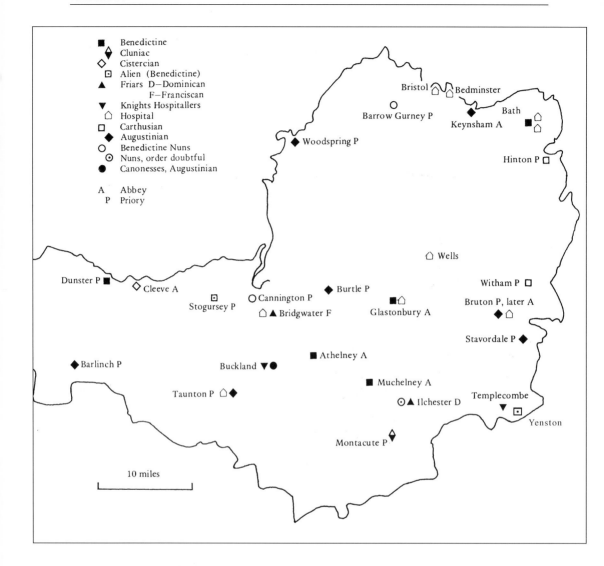

1 The monasteries of Somerset

By that same date arose several other houses, home to canons rather than monks, that is of men whose rule of life was based on the Rule of St Augustine of Hippo which suggested men of missionary outlook. That several of them seem to have developed from the minsters which the Christian Saxon conquerors had introduced is of significance. The houses of canons at Bruton, Keynsham and Taunton, although all three had been formally founded by Norman patrons, inherited and retained characteristics of earlier foundations.

1 A rule for holy living

St Benedict of Nursia (*c*.480-*c*.547), convinced that the only way to escape from the evil of the world was to live in seclusion from it, occupied in religious activities, went at the age of 14 to live in a cave. His later experience of living with other like-minded people led him perhaps *c*.515 to write a book of guidance for religious communities which has come to be known as the Rule of St Benedict.

The Rule recognised the fact that living in a community involved personal discipline and required a formal way of supporting the weak and restraining the over-enthusiastic; a way of encouraging and inspiring the backslider, of developing the skills of the artistic

2   The Rule of St Benedict; a medieval copy now belonging to Wells Cathedral, damaged in antiquity by hot candlewax. Chapter 53, 'on the reception of guests', refers to a separate kitchen for the abbot

and the intellectual so that each member could achieve the spiritual perfection which was its purpose.

Its essence has long been summarised in the three words poverty, chastity and obedience, three characteristics not widely sought and achieved in the twentieth century. They are not to be seen as the purpose of the monastic life but as means to achieve its purpose: a regulated, disciplined community whose aim was the service of God in simplicity and without contact with the world. To that end each member was to be engaged on an average of four hours in worship in choir — the chant and ceremony of the Divine Office — four hours in spiritual reading, prayer and meditation, and some six hours in work which might be domestic or manual.

To follow such a regime the individual had to be lost to the community and the individual will made subservient to the guidance of the superior. The lack of personal possessions described as poverty, the chastity adopted in the acceptance of fellow members of the community as brothers and sisters and superiors as fathers and mothers, and the obedience inherent in the recognition of the Rule offered to very many, both inside and outside those communities, the way of Salvation.

Those communities together nurtured scholars and teachers, craftsmen and artists, spiritual directors and prophets, some of whose words and actions were known far and wide. They were home, by contrast, to men and women of more limited capacities who found in them a secure lodging and rest at the last. And for the majority in between there was the possibility of a fulfilled life of service to God. The monastic life followed by such a wide variety of men and women was an ideal which, in its attempt if not always in its attainment, lay at the heart of England as well as much of Western Europe for close on 600 years.

2 Founders and foundations

Saxon Royal founders

In 1535 every monastery in the land was obliged to answer searching questions about its income and expenditure and the result, known as the *Valor Ecclesiasticus*, gives details of estates and their value. Included under each monastery is a statement of alms given each year to the poor at the request of various benefactors. Bath reckoned to give alms 'to divers poor and leprous people by ancient usage and of the foundation of kings Athelstan, Edgar, Ethelred and Edwy as well as of many other founders'. Muchelney mentioned Centwine, Ine, Athelstan and Ethelred; Athelney regarded Alfred as its 'first founder' and Athelstan, Edgar, Ethelred and Cnut as co-founders and benefactors.

Glastonbury outclassed them all, in the sixteenth century claiming Arthur, Guinevere, Lucius and Prince Yder from a distant age, and the West Saxon kings Cenwealh, Centwine, Ethelwulf, Ethelbald, Ethelred and Edgar. Visitors to the abbey church, of course, had clear evidence of royal support for there were the tombs of Edward the Elder and Edmund Ironside flanking the great black marble tomb of Arthur before the high altar and the copper and gilt effigy of Edgar in its own magnificent chapel beyond.

For those who could read there was, by the end of the fourteenth century, a bold statement of Glastonbury's origins, evidently placed on public display and still surviving on thin oak boards hinged as if once attached, perhaps, to a pillar in the abbey church. In it was the claim to have been founded by Joseph of Arimathia at the request of the Apostle Philip. A variant of that same story declared that Joseph found on arrival a church already standing, dedicated by Christ Himself.

Leaving aside Arthur, the 'king' who proved to be Glastonbury's greatest asset, the Saxon kings of Wessex from Cenwealh (642-72) to Athelstan (924-39) and their successors as kings of England to the time of Cnut (1016-35) were generally remarkable supporters of the monastic ideal. Outstanding among them was Alfred (871-99) whose foundation of Athelney was a deliberate attempt to revive the religious life of his kingdom and provide an educated elite to support his ideas of kingship.

Bath, Athelney, Muchelney and especially Glastonbury all had royal charters among their precious written records, many of them actually forgeries but probably all recording real gifts of land. Some houses also had relics, given them by kings and others, and the memory of those ancient origins was to be revived in some Benedictine houses at the beginning of the sixteenth century. Among the monks of Bath who surrendered in 1539 were three who on taking their vows had been given new names in religion: John Browne had become John Athelstan, John Sodbury had changed to John Edgar, Edward Style to Edward Edwy. Monks called John Edgar, Richard Athelstan and Richard Alfred were at Athelney in 1534, and at Glastonbury were a Centwine, an Ine, an Athelstan and an Edgar.

3 *Glastonbury abbey: the site of Arthur's tomb*

The name of Dunstan was taken by three Glastonbury monks, and while he cannot be regarded as a founder of the house in a legal or political sense, yet surely his introduction of the Rule of St Benedict to Glastonbury when he became abbot *c*.943 was a vital part of the revival of monastic life in England after what seems to have been virtual collapse in the face of Viking invasions a century earlier.

> (Dunstan) decided that he would occupy himself with manual labour in addition to the daily exercise of singing . . . [and] in order to have some sort of workshop, he built a little shed with a lean-to roof next to the church of the Mother of God. There he applied his hands to his work, his lips to the psalms, and his mind to heaven. The stylus ran over the surface of the tablet, the pen over the page. He took up the brush to paint and the chisel to carve. Indeed, in Glastonbury there are, according to tradition, altarcloths, crosses, thuribles, phials, chasubles and other vestments of his workmanship.

So John of Glastonbury recorded the tradition of his house in the fourteenth century. St Benedict could have had no finer pupil and Glastonbury and the Benedictine Order in England no finer exemplar.

4   *Glastonbury abbey: the* Magna
     Tabula, *the fourteenth-century guide
     book*

The Norman founders of the conquest

Among the leading followers of William the Conqueror who were given land in Somerset were William de Mohun and Walter or Walschin of Douai. William de Mohun, who came from Moyon near St Lo not far from Cherbourg, held in 1086 a group of estates near the sea in West Somerset centred on his castle of Dunster, a strategic position from which he could defend the coast from possible invasion by surviving members of the conquered Saxon royal house.

Walter of Douai, evidently an expert castle builder, was given land much more widely dispersed in the county, where he could similarly defend the rest of Somerset from invasion from the Channel by sea and river. So he was lord of Bridgwater, Burnham and Worle, of East Harptree and (Castle) Cary and Wincanton, and on most of those a castle was built. He also had a castle near Wincanton, but just over the border in Wiltshire, from which a strong defence of the county could be made at the southern end of Selwood Forest; and his principal castle was just over the Devon border at Bampton.

Those two Norman soldiers did what was expected of conquerors on behalf of their lord the king, but they were not simply soldiers; they were also men who had a lively concern for their immortal souls. So between 1090 and 1100 William, 'pricked by the fear of God' and for the benefit of his own soul, the soul of the king, and the souls of his ancestors and successors, gave the church of Dunster, which he requested be 'built and raised', and the tithes of much of his land to the Benedictine monks of Bath. Adelisa his wife agreed to the arrangement, and among the witnesses to his charter were Geoffrey and Robert, his younger sons, and his brother Wilmund. It was clearly a family affair, the first of several grants of land to monasteries by the Mohuns of Dunster.

Walter of Douai made a similar grant of land to the Bath monks in a transaction which involved his wife, his sons, his brother Raimar and his steward Gerard. Walter's gift was the church at Bampton in Devon, not far from his castle, and was 'for his soul and for a burial place in the abbey'. The rest of the grant included the church of Bridgwater and half the tithes of (Castle) Cary given by Walter's wife and sons, the church and land at Bratton (Seymour) given by Gerard, and land called Foxcume given by Raimar. Walter died *c.*1107 and on the day of his burial at Bath his heir Robert of Bampton confirmed the validity of the gifts. The monks, for their part, presented Walter's widow with 60 shillings and a missal.

Foundations continue

5   The seal of Montacute priory, showing the Virgin flanked by SS Peter and Paul

A second generation of Norman landowners continued the tradition, either introducing one of the new and stricter Orders from the continent, and thus planting foreign monks on English soil, or actually endowing their own favourite monastery at home with some of their newly-acquired land.

The greatest magnate in Somerset by the time Domesday Book was compiled in 1086 was the Conqueror's half-brother Robert, count of Mortain. He himself had been unhappy with the succession of William Rufus to the English throne on the Conqueror's death in 1087 and had rebelled in the following year. He died in 1090 and his son William took up arms against Henry I. In 1106 William was taken prisoner at the battle of Tinchebrai and all his lands were forfeit. Thereafter he spent many years in prison but died as a monk of the Cluniac house of Bermondsey.

Both Robert and William have been associated with the foundation of Montacute priory, the first and only Cluniac house in Somerset — Robert indirectly because of the record of the death of the first prior about 1078; William because of the priory's earliest charters which name him as founder. But those charters are forgeries whose irregularity suggests that the arrival of the monks was closely connected with William's disgrace, possibly as some sort of expiation for his crimes. That is more a matter for speculation than certainty. The charters themselves tell in general a common story: that the original gift of lands on the vast Mortain estate was made by Count William and his men to the great abbey of Cluny, and that Cluny sent over a community of monks to establish a house in the earliest years of the twelfth century. Among the places in Somerset and Dorset from which the monks drew their income were Bishopston (part of Montacute), Thorne, Bickenhall, Chinnock and Melbury, the holdings of Bretel de St Clair, Richard son of Drew, William de Lestre, Ansger the Breton, Mauger de Cartrai and Alfred the butler, men

6 *Montacute priory: the site below the* mons acutus *where the former castle stood*

7 *Stogursey priory church: the choir in the early nineteenth century*

whose names suggest that they, too, came from across the English Channel, all evidently members of Count William's feudal entourage.

There was a similar cross-Channel situation at Stogursey where at some date between 1100 and 1107 William de Falaise, a native of the Conqueror's own birthplace, and his wife Geva, the heiress of the estate, gave the church and its tithes to the Benedictine abbey of Lonlay in their native Normandy. They also gave tithes of other nearby land, some essential pasture on the Quantock hills, and also tithes in Devon and South Wales. Members of the community at Lonlay sent over to administer those possessions became, by *c.*1120, a small religious community; never so large as Montacute and never so independent of their mother house in France. That and poverty in the end proved their downfall.

But before that time the founder's kin had continued their support for the monks. William de Curci, steward of Henry II's household, confirmed to the monks the gifts of William de Falaise his great-grandfather, William de Curci his grandfather, and William de Curci his father. Among other neighbouring landowners who also gave, or possibly sold, property to the monks within the first 50 years of foundation were members of the Columbers and FitzUrse families, including Reginald FitzUrse, one of the murderers of Archbishop Thomas Becket.

The priory (later abbey) at Bruton was, for a time, a house with lands on both sides of the English Channel. In 1142 William de Mohun of Dunster, who had been created earl of Somerset by Empress Matilda for supporting her against King Stephen, issued a charter addressed to Bishop Robert of Bath. He did so at the request of William the chaplain, with the advice of his wife and of many friends and vassals, and for the redemption of his sins. By the charter he gave to the community of Augustinian canons at Bruton all the property William the chaplain held there, together with common pasture in his own manor of Brewham. Exactly who William the chaplain was will probably never be known, but the church which the canons already held was probably in origin a Saxon minster church. The canons certainly regarded William de Mohun as their founder, and some 40 years later another William de Mohun confirmed the grants of his father and grandfather and also the grants made by some of his family's tenants, including Robert FitzGeoffrey, who had given the church of Luxborough in his grandfather's time, and others with distinctly Norman names, such as Henry de Careville, Alexander de Cantelou, and Ralph de Tankerville. For his own part William gave to the canons some more property in England and some ancestral possessions in Normandy, which the canons were later to exchange with Troarn abbey near Caen for Troarn's English lands in Sussex and Gloucestershire. The property in England included a mill at Minehead, which was given to the canons, in the usual phrase, for the love of God and the salvation of his soul, and specifically to provide them with a special meal on the anniversary of his death each year if he died returning on pilgrimage from Jerusalem. He probably did.

At the same time William de Mohun allowed the canons the right to choose a prior from among themselves rather than have him appoint the head of the house, on condition that the man so chosen should present himself to William and his successors as patrons of the priory.

The founder's reward for all this generosity was the knowledge that the canons prayed for him and his family and offered them burial in their church. A noble tomb might be a benefit in its turn. Sir John de Mohun, eldest son of Sir Reynold de Mohun, died in Gascony during his father's lifetime, probably between 1252 and 1254. His heart was buried before the high altar of the Cistercian abbey at Newenham in Devon which his father had only recently founded. The rest of the corpse was thereafter sent on its way to Salisbury for burial but was seized by the prior of Bruton and buried instead in his church, for which boldness he had to apologise to Salisbury's dean and chapter. The monks of Bath also undertook to say Mass for all time for the souls of both Sir John and his father in the castle chapel at Dunster.

The Augustinian canons of Taunton looked not to a lay magnate but to a bishop as their founder, but in a real sense that bishop, William Giffard, was a greater magnate than most and the huge estate at Taunton was one of his extensive possessions. The house of secular canons may well have been successor to a Saxon minster, but the date of its own foundation was perhaps never precisely recorded. Bishop Giffard's part is sufficiently well agreed and the date is between 1120 and 1125. Giffard's successor, Henry of Blois, added to the endowment and in fact provided a better site than the one inherited from the minster, by that time in embarrassingly close proximity to the bishop's castle. So Giffard and Henry of Blois were regarded as the two founders of the priory though by 1334 the canons' archives included as many as 130 charters recording grants of land and other rights from many benefactors.

Keynsham, probably the second of the larger houses of Augustinian canons, emerged from a family tragedy. Robert, the heir to the great Earl William of Gloucester, died at the age of 16 in 1166 and was buried on the family manor of Keynsham. The boy had asked his father to found a monastery for the salvation of his soul, and in the following year the pope approved the plan in a letter to Roger, bishop of Worcester, the boy's uncle. The house was to be at Keynsham for regular canons and was to be for the souls of the bishop's ancestors and especially for Robert himself. The house was formally opened some time between May 1172 and the following April.

8   *The seal of Stephen, prior of Bruton, probably Stephen of Kari, removed 1255. The prior is the suppliant at the feet of the Virgin Mary*

9   *The seal of the priory of SS Peter and Paul, Taunton*

Cleve Abbey, Somersetshire.

10 *Cleve abbey in the eighteenth century*

The new orders: Cistercians and Carthusians

The first (and only) Cistercian house in Somerset did not appear until the end of the great century of monastic foundation, largely because of the opposition, while he was bishop between 1136 and 1166, of the Cluniac Robert of Lewes. When it came, at some date between 1186 and 1191, it was in the parish of (Old) Cleve on the initiative of William de Roumare, earl of Lincoln, the Benniworth family, and William's successor Hubert de Burgh, one of King John's strongest supporters. All were Lincolnshire folk and the monks who came to the new house were already members of the Cistercian community at Revesby in Lincolnshire, an abbey founded by William de Roumare's grandfather.

The murder of Archbishop Becket in 1170 had at least three consequences in Somerset. Reginald FitzUrse, one of the murderers, gave up half his manor of Williton to the Knights Templar as a way of raising money to travel to Rome and the Holy Land to do penance. His grandson William de Courtenay founded the house of Augustinian canons at Woodspring based on a chapel he had already built in honour of the Blessed Thomas.

The third consequence was more direct. Henry II's inability to travel as a pilgrim to Palestine in order to obtain absolution for his part in Thomas's death was commuted to the foundation of religious houses, one of which, at Witham, was to be the first Carthusian house in England.

In fact more is known about the foundation of Witham than about any other house in Somerset: references about the financial aspects of the foundation from the payments recorded in the Pipe Rolls of the royal exchequer and, quite remarkably, the evidence of the original charter of foundation, found by chance among the papers of a Shropshire solicitor in 1918 and now kept in the cathedral library at Wells. The charter is marked on the reverse with the letter 'A', its index mark in the archives of the monastery and once the most cherished possession of the house.

In addition to the substantial sums paid for building during the period 1179-80 to 1186-7, in the financial year Michaelmas 1179 to Michaelmas 1180 the sheriff of Somerset and Dorset was relieved of the charge of £10 from Witham 'where the brethren of the Carthusian Order reside' and the sheriff of Hampshire produced £13 6s 8d 'for buying clothing for the brethren'. In 1181-2 £10 was given 'for seed to sow the land', £10 for lengths of cloth, 27s for 'nine ells of blanket', and £80 for food, in 1182-3 £6 13s 4d on clothing, in 1185-6 £20 for clothing and other necessaries, in 1186-7 62s 6d for corn.

11 The foundation charter of Witham priory, 1183

The site on which those buildings appeared was a remote one on royal land in Selwood Forest where tenants had to be compensated with land elsewhere. In spite of evident royal generosity and the issue of a formal charter of foundation in September 1186, the success of the venture was in some doubt. The first prior, Norbert, sent from the mother house in Burgundy returned home in despair; the second died in England, presumably *c*.1178-9. The invitation from the king to Hugh of Avalon brought a remarkable man to England and to Witham *c*.1180 where he found monks living in 'cells built of logs, in a small valley and surrounded by an enclosure of pales'.

Under Hugh and with the support of the king a monastery was successfully established where solitude and contemplation were guaranteed in the little cells arranged around one large cloister and where lay brothers

12 The common seal of the house of the Blessed Mary of Witham

13 Hinton priory: the chapter house and library

in the nearby settlement of Witham Friary (from *frererie*) worked the land which provided the monks' food.

The date of Somerset's second Carthusian house is also known almost precisely: on the same day in May between 1226 and 1230, when the widowed Countess Ela of Salisbury founded both the house of nuns at Lacock and the monastery at Hinton. Monks already established at Hatherop in Gloucestershire by her husband William Longespée were transferred to the new house where later the community was to make a name for itself for learning and piety and where many of its buildings still survive.

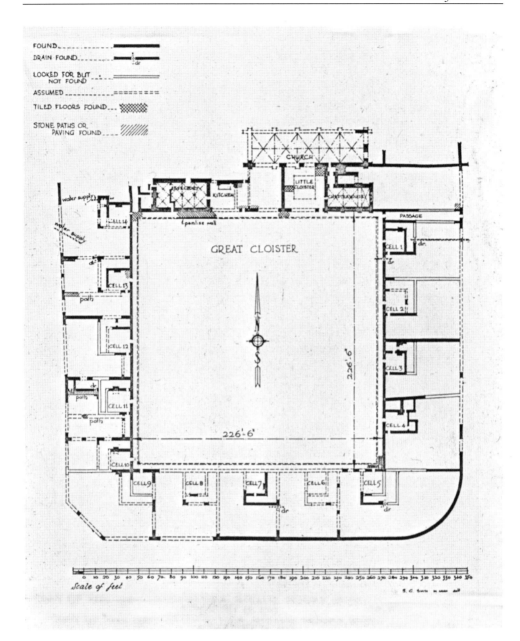

FOUND
DRAIN FOUND
LOOKED FOR BUT
   NOT FOUND
ASSUMED
TILED FLOORS FOUND
STONE PATHS OR
   PAVING FOUND

CHURCH

REFECTORY   KITCHEN   LITTLE
                      CLOISTER   CHAPTERHOUSE

water supply

CELL 14

PASSAGE

CELL 1   dr

GREAT CLOISTER

CELL 13
path

226'.6"

CELL 2

CELL 12

CELL 3

CELL 11
path
path

CELL 4

226'.6"

CELL 10

CELL 5

CELL 9   CELL 8   CELL 7   CELL 6   dr

0 10 20 30 40 50 60 70 80 90 100 110 120 130 140 150 160 170 180 190 200 210 220 230 240 250 260 270 280 290 300 310 320 330 340 350
Scale of feet

14 Hinton priory, plan

Nunneries and hospitals

The small and poor Somerset nunneries could not compare with the more famous houses just over the Wiltshire and Dorset boundary at Amesbury, Lacock or Shaftesbury, and their economic poverty was matched by the paucity of their records. Probably Robert de Curci founded Cannington during the second quarter of the twelfth century and Hawise de Gournay established the house at Barrow *c.*1200. Minchin Buckland is better documented, but its complicated history as the only house for ladies of the Order of St John of Jerusalem was due at least in part to William de Erlegh, also *c.*1200.

One final group of foundations were hospitals, whose founders were a mixture of lay and clerical. Perhaps the earliest was St John's in Bath, established by Bishop Reginald in 1180. The other clerical founders were the Wells brothers, Hugh and Jocelin. Hugh, formerly archdeacon of Wells and from 1209 bishop elect of Lincoln, but in exile for his opposition to King John, drew up a will in 1212 in which he gave 500 marks towards building a hospital at Wells and small sums to St John's, Bath, and to leper houses outside Bath and Ilchester. Hugh's brother Jocelin, bishop of Bath from 1206, added more endowment for the Wells hospital. An abbot of Glastonbury was presumably founder of St John's hospital there before 1235. Of the secular founders, William Brewer endowed St John's hospital, Bridgwater, Robert de Berkeley St Katherine's at Bedminster, William Dacus that at Ilchester, and John Farcey St John's, Redcliffe.

3 Patrons and patronage

In the three centuries and more of monastic life after the first flush of foundations the descendants of founders continued to be involved, usually at rather a distance, with the work of their ancestors. Glastonbury, Muchelney and Athelney, as was only sensible, paid due respect to the king when an abbot died and a new one had to be found. The cathedral priory and St John's hospital, both in Bath, and St John's hospital at Wells all rightly looked to the bishop as patron as well as diocesan, for he was, after all, titular abbot of the first, and his predecessors Reginald and Jocelin were either founders or co-founders of the other two. So, for example, Bishop Bekynton in 1447 gave licence for the monks of Bath to choose a successor to William Southbroke. Interestingly, the bishop not only sent his formal permission; he also wrote a letter to the monks, telling them they should choose a man of God, not someone who would give way to the prayers or threats of the powerful in such a sacred matter as was now before them. The same bishop's vicar-general gave permission in 1462 for the election of a new master of Wells hospital.

The Cluniacs of Montacute saw their situation differently and war between England and France produced complications for a house which regarded Cluny as its mother and the abbot of Cluny as father-in-God. War brought such ties into conflict with the English Crown. Edward III first took the house into his own patronage but in 1339 he granted it to William de Montagu, earl of Salisbury, himself descendant of a man who took his name from the village. In the following year, although he himself was abroad, Earl William's attornies appointed the Englishman John de Henton as the new prior in place of the obviously foreign Guichard Jou. Montacute thereafter was a truly English house and by the early fifteenth century no longer dependent on Cluny, normally choosing its own prior with no outside interference. In 1458, however, William Waynflete, bishop of Winchester, appointed a new prior on the death of Prior Robert Montague. The bishop had presumably been asked for his opinion by the convent, perhaps because they could not find a suitable candidate from among themselves; he chose Robert Newton, then a monk at Glastonbury, and the unusual choice was assented to by a man who presumably considered himself the priory's patron, James Butler, earl of Wiltshire, a distant descendant of William de Montagu.

The Luttrells, successors to the Mohuns at Dunster, continued the connection with Bruton. The Luttrells still in the fourteenth century accepted as an ancient custom the gift of two wax candles to light their chamber whenever they stayed overnight with the canons. Among their archives the Luttrells, like the Mohuns before them, kept letters the canons sent each time their prior died, seeking permission for the election of another. There is a letter for every election between 1255 and 1532.

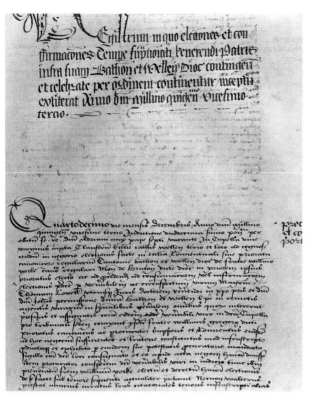

15 William Yorke, canon of Bruton, is elected prior of Taunton, 1523

On the death of William, earl of Gloucester and founder of Keynsham, in 1183 the earldom passed into the possession first of his grandson, then of his youngest daughter, and from 1217 to another grandson, Gilbert de Clare. The Clares were more interested in other houses and tended to ignore Keynsham, but their eventual heirs, the earls of Stafford, regarded their patronage of Keynsham as a piece of real estate in the late fourteenth century and their successors did so in the fifteenth. In 1456 Humphrey Stafford, duke of Buckingham and earl of Hereford, Stafford and Northampton, not only granted the prior and convent licence to elect a new abbot on the resignation of Walter Bekynsfeld, but also sent a letter to the bishop notifying him that he as patron consented to the election of Thomas Tyler. Through his marriage to the widow of Henry, earl of Stafford, Jasper Tudor, duke of Bedford, left instructions in his will for his burial at Keynsham at his death in 1495 and the grave vault has been tentatively identified by archaeologists.

Bishops of Winchester retained their formal links with the canons of Taunton: Bishop Droxford in 1326, for instance, wrote to Bishop John Stratford of Winchester announcing that he, as diocesan, had confirmed the election of Ralph of Culmstock as the new prior. Early in 1476 the then bishop of Winchester, William Waynflete, not only gave permission for the canons to proceed to an election on the death of Prior Richard Gleve, but in the event found himself making the choice when the canons made over the right to him. First the canons informed their patron that their prior had died on 31 January. On 19 February they met in their chapter house and decided on 22 February as the day of the election. The

16 Stavordale priory, the Jesus chapel

17 Richard Whiting is confirmed as abbot of Glastonbury by Cardinal Wolsey, 1525

15 members of the community, with an adviser, scribes and witnesses, after mass and a sermon, received the patron's licence to elect and then decided that he should make the decision himself. From his manor house at Bishop's Waltham Waynflete sent a formal document dated 27 February, nominating one of the younger members, John Ayssh. The community met again on 7 March, having received the patron's nomination, formally announced the result to people assembled in the priory church, and finally told the nominee himself. He, as modesty required, 'craved time for consideration', but after an hour accepted. The patron would not have cared for a refusal.

It is possible that some of the smaller and poorer houses had no patrons in such a formal, legal sense, though on the occasion of an election for the mastership of St John's hospital, Bridgwater, in 1457 the community were wise to report the loss of their master to the joint lords of the town, Richard Plantagenet, duke of York, and Edmund Zouche, Lord Zouche, direct successors of the first founder, William Brewer. More than 60 years later the brethren reported the death of another master to the then owners of Bridgwater, none other than Queen Katherine of Aragon, who held one third of the town as part of her jointure, and Henry Daubeney, Baron Daubeney, later to parade himself as earl of Bridgwater.

Richard Seymour, successor to the Lovels, lords of Castle Cary, was acknowledged to be the patron of Stavordale priory, although neither the date of its foundation nor the name of its founder have survived. Richard's great-granddaughter Alice, wife of William Zouche, Baron Zouche, brought the patronage to her husband's family although John Stourton, in generously leaving enough money to rebuild part of the monastery in 1439, may have been making a bid as a rival and was buried under the tower of the priory church. However, Alice Seymour's grandson John, Baron Zouche, seems to have found a home in the buildings of the house and directed burial for himself in the Jesus chapel on the north side of the canons' choir.

By the sixteenth century many of the historic patrons had had their day and Humphrey Stafford, probably a natural son of Henry Stafford, was one of many whose claim to what they regarded as their hereditary right was not acknowledged. In spite of his

18 Stavordale priory, the former priory church

father's position as founder of Woodspring priory, his own claims to acquire it were ignored when the house was dissolved in 1536.

For there were others whose connections with houses were more practical. For ten years and more most monasteries had been looking out for protectors who would either save them from poverty or from the increasing threat to their continued existence. Between 1523 and 1527 the absence of the diocesan bishop on diplomatic missions abroad may have induced Taunton, Barlinch, Bath, Athelney, and even Glastonbury to turn to Cardinal Wolsey, not for cash but for new abbots or priors, and probably for the political support which their requests implied.

The case of Glastonbury was particularly surprising. Abbot Richard Bere died on 20 January 1525. The congé d'élire from the Crown, the licence to choose his successor, was issued on 1 February. A month later, evidently after negotiations between the community and Wolsey, the monks agreed to delegate their responsibility to the cardinal. The formal election of Richard Whiting took place in Wolsey's private chapel at York Place. Just over a month later that election was confirmed by Wolsey's commissioners.

Whether Whiting would have been the free choice of the monks will never be known. He was probably nearly 50 years of age and had served two administrative offices: receiver of casuals and chamberlain. He was thus mature and experienced, but did Wolsey see him as pliant? The suspicion is strengthened when, by September 1529, the office of chief steward of the abbey was held by the government's leading lawyer Sir Thomas More.

At that date More was Chancellor of the Duchy of Lancaster; two months later he became Lord Chancellor when Wolsey fell, and he remained chief steward after his own fall from favour at least until October 1532. For obvious political reasons Whiting could not have retained him for much longer. His successor as steward was the Taunton lawyer Sir William Portman.

By the 1530s the whole body of religious was clearly nervous; debts, poor recruitment and political pressures both locally and from the king's government were diverting monks and nuns from their purpose. Among the fees payable by the last abbot of Athelney were sums of between 13s 4d and 40s each to local gentry, legal advisers and local royal officials, and one of 53s 4d to 'Master Secretary'.

It was to this same Master Secretary, Thomas Cromwell, that Richard Zouche wrote, hinting heavily that since Stavordale was virtually empty and since it was of his family's inheritance, then he might be permitted to acquire it. It was to this same Master Secretary that Sir John FitzJames wrote to prevent the expected election of a new abbot at Bruton and to arrange for the choice of one more amenable. It was to the same that Abbot Dovell of Cleeve wrote for permission to travel from his house to administer its estates; to the same that Abbot Yve wrote from Muchelney about the £100 he paid to Cromwell to secure his election; and that same man received each year from Muchelney 66s 8d and from the monks of Montacute £4. Thomas Cromwell, formerly secretary to Wolsey and later the man who masterminded the dissolution of the monasteries for Henry VIII, had more than a passing personal interest in keeping them open.

The benefits for founders

Once established with adequate buildings and sufficient endowment, a monastic community could get on with its primary task, the regular round of work and worship required by its Order. How far the founder and his kin made demands after the first flush of enthusiasm is difficult to know, but the spiritual advantages of having a religious community in their midst were clearly recognised by neighbours. The knowledge that prayers were regularly said and masses sung in monastic churches when similar prayers might be bought in chantry foundations in parish and cathedral churches indicates the continuing attraction of at least some monasteries. Thus while the grant of some land in Ilton to Athelney by Alexander de Pirou in the later twelfth century for the soul of Richard de Montacute and for the safety of his own soul and of

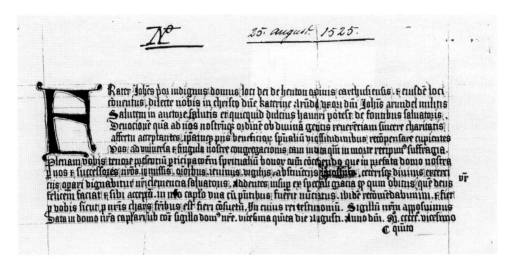

19 *Letter of confraternity of John, prior of Hinton, to Katherine, wife of Sir John Arundell, 1525*

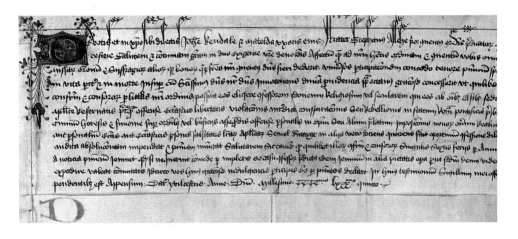

20 *Stephen Assche, prior of the Dominicans of Ilchester, grants confraternity to John Kendall and his wife Matilda, 1485*

that of his son William was one of many hundreds whereby monasteries increased their original endowments, the grant of William Botreaux, Lord Botreaux, to Bath in 1458 suggests that his faith not only in the efficacy of prayer but in the monks' ability to perform it was undiminished.

In 1458, in return for a grant to them of property in Yeovilton and Camerton, the community at Bath undertook to say mass each day for the good estate of King Henry VI, Queen Margaret his wife, and Edward, Prince of Wales, and also for the good estate of the donor and his wife while they lived and for their souls after death. The agreement between Lord Botreaux and the monks was extremely detailed, describing the liturgy of each mass and directing mention by the celebrant not only of the names of the king, queen and prince and of Lord and Lady Botreaux, but also Lord Botreaux' first wife, his parents and his grandparents, for anyone else he might name in writing to the celebrant, for the souls of all his ancestors and, indeed, for all Christian souls. One copy of this fascinating agreement was still preserved by the founder's descendant, the earl of Huntingdon, in the eighteenth century, long after the agreement itself had become null and void when the monks left Bath.

Lord Botreaux was more than conventionally pious, perhaps influenced, like Earl William of Gloucester before him, by the loss of his only son. He was also a little unusual for his time in turning to the Benedictines, but like many of his contemporaries he was also attracted to the Franciscans. He and his wife were remembered as 'especial benefactors' to the Franciscans at Bridgwater and his heart and his wife's body were buried in the friars' church where, long before, the bodies of his son and daughter had been translated from their original tombs at North Cadbury. From the same social class was Sir Thomas Brooke (d.1439) whose widow endowed masses for themselves and two members of the Cheddar family at Barlinch.

Mutual benefits might also be offered by means of confraternity. In 1479 the guardian of the Franciscans at Bridgwater issued letters declaring in resounding language that John Kendall, his wife and two children, Marmaduke Lumley, and William Kendall had been enrolled. The names were added to each of the letters, which were formally sealed. Kendall and his wife were similarly enrolled among the confraters of the Dominicans at Ilchester in 1485 in a fine piece of writing whose initial letter is illuminated in red, blue, green and gold. No doubt confraternity had its price as well as benefits.

By the fifteenth century new permanent endowments had become few and far between, but the wills of increasing numbers of lay people of modest means from the fifteenth century include relatively small sums of cash and other gifts made to the friars at Ilchester and Bridgwater, to houses of nuns and to the Carthusians at Hinton and Witham. In return testators requested prayers and occasionally burial rights. So in 1444 William Balsham the elder of Ilchester left the friars there 13s 4d so that he might be buried in their church, together with sums of 12d to each friar who was a priest and 6d to each of the rest of the community in return for the prayers of them all and the recitation of the psalter by each priest. Each sister at Buckland was to receive 6d and their house 6s 8d, also in return for recitation of the psalter. Alice, William's widow, survived until 1457 and then left a cloth of gold pall in payment for her burial in the friary.

In his will dated 1503 John Fox wished to be buried at the entrance to the cloister at Witham and gave the monks 40s and a silver goblet. He also left money to the church in the nearby village and to the monks' servants.

David Cornishe, a merchant of Combwich, asked the nuns of Cannington and the brethren of St John's hospital at Bridgwater to pray for him and left cash to the Franciscans of Bridgwater. Only the sisters of Barrow Gurney seem to have done rather poorly.

4 Fathers in God

The bishops of the Somerset diocese, calling themselves first of Wells and later of Bath, were latecomers in comparison with the monasteries at Glastonbury, Bath, Muchelney and Athelney, but the relationship, for instance, between Dunstan and the new cathedral at Wells was evidently more than cordial and recognised the primacy of the bishop and his clergy. Thus what came to be known as the Gift of St Dunstan, the offering from Glastonbury of bread, mead, and two small pigs or kids, was recognition that Dunstan himself saw Wells as the mother church of the diocese and its bishop as his Father in God.

The appearance of new houses and new monastic Orders from the time of the foundation of Montacute onwards coincided with the growth of the power of bishops and the beginnings of a formal and organised system of episcopal government. Bishop Robert of Lewes (1136-66), himself a Cluniac monk personally opposed to the Cistercians, not only rebuilt his cathedral at Wells but made it the heart of his government. The changed status of Bath, no longer having his episcopal seat, may have raised the question of his relationship with other religious houses, though as a protégé of Henry of Blois, whom he had served first as prior of Winchester and later as administrator of Glastonbury, relations with Glastonbury would hardly have been difficult.

Both bishops must have been conscious that the increasing power of the new cathedral at Wells might need careful handling and both were clear about the threat posed to the rather staid and wealthy Benedictines by the more enthusiastic and more rigorous views of their own Cluniac Order and even more of the Cistercians. Henry, if not initiating the search for a biblical founder for Glastonbury, evidently gave the movement his blessing and it was almost certainly in his time that in the rewriting of Glastonbury's early history there emerged a charter of King Ine dated 725. This excluded the bishop from the abbey and its immediate vicinity without the permission of the abbot, restricted him, if invited, to no more than three attendants, and required him and his clerks at Wells to honour Glastonbury as their mother church by singing the litany on the Monday after the Ascension. The charter was, of course, a forgery.

The successors of Henry and Robert significantly altered the balance. The new abbot was Robert, formerly prior of Winchester; the new bishop was Reginald FitzJocelin, a man with powerful political connections. Bishop Reginald began a new cathedral at Wells, the one still surviving, on a larger scale perhaps to make clear that spiritual leadership in the diocese lay with the bishop. Nevertheless, his relations with Bath remained friendly and he himself was to be buried there in 1191 after his untimely death soon after his election as archbishop of Canterbury. Reginald had, incidentally, been directly involved in bringing Hugh of Avalon from Burgundy to Witham and was one of the supporters for Hugh's promotion to be bishop of Lincoln, possibly because Hugh's great influence in the West Country was becoming a potential threat to his own spiritual position.

21 Glastonbury, the eastern crossing piers of the great church

More important from the bishop's standpoint were the claims of Glastonbury to special rights over seven churches in and around the abbey. Founded on the forged charter of Ine and another from King Edgar, an independent archdeaconry of Glastonbury was created, to be ruled by the abbey. In exchange for his approval the bishop was given by the abbey the churches of Pilton and South Brent. Pilton passed to the cathedral, part of it forming a prebend to be held by successive abbots of Glastonbury who, although not required to live at Wells like most prebendaries, still became members of the bishop's cathedral chapter. Later Glastonbury historians saw this agreement as a great mistake, for by accepting it the bishop's subservient role in the forged charter had been reversed. Bishop Reginald's successor recognised its value, and in his time the abbots of Muchelney and Athelney also became members of the Wells chapter. Reginald's agreement with Glastonbury was confirmed in 1179 by Pope Alexander III and among the rights mentioned was the Gift of St Dunstan, a clear contradiction of the claims of the Ine charter.

Reginald's successor, Savaric FitzGeldewin (1192-1205), overreached himself in his relationship with Glastonbury although he was clearly not the only bishop wishing to curb the increasing independence of monasteries. Using his family connections with the Holy Roman Emperor and the power he had in negotiations for the release of Richard I, he first took Reginald's place as bishop of Bath and then, having failed to secure the vacant archbishopric of Canterbury, took over Glastonbury, whose abbot had recently left at the bishop's request.

So began 40 years of acute rivalry between Wells and Glastonbury; of orders and counter-orders from popes, kings and archbishops; of a rival abbot at Glastonbury; of excommunications and threats; and in 1199 of Savaric's invasion of the house when the monks were first shut up in the infirmary and later forced by means ranging between beatings and promises to sign a declaration to the pope accepting Savaric as their abbot.

Trouble naturally broke out again on Savaric's death in 1205. Petitions, evidently encouraged by King John, came from many sources including the abbeys of Bath and Muchelney and the canons of Wells deploring the effect of the past few years on the spiritual and economic state of Glastonbury. The new bishop, Jocelin of Wells, had been much involved as a canon of the cathedral with the early stages of the union of see and abbey and was evidently reluctant to make changes to a scheme for which he had once held high hopes. He was supported by the powerful Pope Innocent III, but after Innocent's death his successor was able to reverse the policy and Jocelin and the monks came to an understanding. Jocelin agreed to the end of the union between the see and the abbey and freedom of the monks to elect their own abbot; in their turn the monks gave up some land. The bishop was still in many ways supreme; no longer bishop of Bath and Glastonbury (from 1219 he was known as bishop of Bath) Jocelin was still the abbey's patron, taking the abbey into his control when an abbot died, granting permission to the monks to elect a new abbot, confirming that election, blessing the new abbot, having the right of visitation and acting as the abbey's feudal lord in respect of estates it held of the Crown. The abbey's historians disliked Jocelin almost as much as Savaric for his reluctance to give back all that Glastonbury had claimed.

The struggle between the bishops and Glastonbury was not over. It was probably an irritant to the bishop that William of St Vigor, like Henry de Sully before him as abbot, was permitted by the pope to wear the mitre and other trappings of a bishop. Disagreement among the monks on William's death in 1223 allowed Bishop Jocelin to impose his own candidate in Robert, formerly prior of Bath. Robert's successor, Michael of Amesbury, may well have retired in the face of some aggressive moves by Bishop William of Bitton (I) (1248-64) who in 1253 exercised his role as feudal lord by levying a tax on the abbey tenants, and in 1255 as visitor he deposed Abbot Roger of Ford. Appeals to king and pope against the bishop proved expensive for the abbey and finally a compromise was reached with Bitton's successor, the powerful Walter Giffard, who yielded the right to be the abbey's feudal lord in return for some more of the abbey's lands. The second Bishop William of Bitton (1267-74) and his successor Robert Burnell (1275-92) were both involved in the question of the abbey's patronage. Burnell evidently used his friendship with the king to secure adequate compensation in land for the loss of his claim as patron.

John Droxford or Drokensford came to Wells after distinguished government service as controller and later keeper of the wardrobe and acting royal treasurer between 1290 and 1309 when he had been at the heart of the administration of the military and diplomatic activities of both Edward I and for a short time of Edward II. When he came to Wells a year after his consecration he was new to the office of bishop and had to make his mark. At Glastonbury and Bath were Abbot Geoffrey Fromund and Prior Robert Clopcote, two men well established in their respective houses and prepared to challenge the new bishop's authority.

Early in 1313, therefore, the bishop formally opened visitations at Bath, at his cathedral in Wells and at Glastonbury. The opening ceremonies involved demands that each member should answer questions about the state of the community and hide nothing, and the bishop felt obliged to issue a formal warning to the prior, the dean and the abbot, on no account to try to cover up the truth by administering oaths of secrecy to their brethren. In the event, although no record of formal visitation proceedings has survived, despite a space left in the bishop's register for the purpose, Abbot Fromund was probably able to retain the independence his predecessors had fought so hard to achieve. Still, the bishop could conduct an inquiry into the orders of priests holding benefices within the abbey's archdeaconry; and ten years later, at the beginning of Abbot Adam of Sodbury's rule, he consecrated the rebuilt parish church of Meare. As for Bath, Bishop Droxford found in the 1320s that Prior Clopcote had wasted the priory's income, perhaps in his attempt to raise his own status by asking the pope for the right to use the mitre and crosier of a bishop. Ever since 1295 the priors of Bath had sat with bishops and others including the abbots of Glastonbury in the nation's Great Councils and Parliaments. The finances of the priory were evidently unable to bear the charges of such a position and the monks found themselves short of food. Bishop Droxford at least was able to restore financial stability and early in 1326 accepted the profession of 13 new monks, four of whom were recorded simply as John and three as William.

Muchelney was visited in 1315 and again in 1328, Stavordale in 1322 and evidence of mismanagement at nunneries at Ilchester, Barrow and Cannington brought action from the bishop: the Ilchester sisters were said to have been starving because of mismanagement, the prioress of Barrow was removed, and some of the nuns of

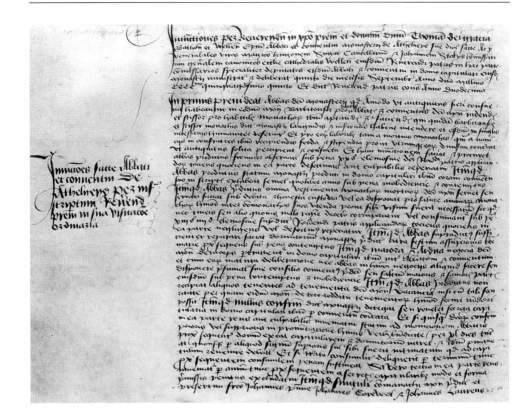

22 Bishop Thomas Bekynton and his visitors issue injunctions to Athelney abbey 1455

Cannington were wandering abroad. But all was not discipline and correction. Droxford was willing to support the monks of Athelney in their need to raise money for their buildings and urged a swift election for a new prior at Barlinch to save costs.

Ralph of Shrewsbury (1329-63), Nicholas Bubwith (1407-24) and John Stafford (1425-43) each exercised authority over Somerset's religious houses as their office required, removing unsatisfactory heads, reproving slackness, encouraging and supporting the needy. Bishop Ralph, for instance, allowed the canons of Stavordale to collect alms in the diocese for two years from 1335 to complete their church and offered indulgences to the generous; Bishop Nicholas in 1412 warned the aged Margery FitzNichol, formerly prioress of Barrow, that she was not to neglect worship according to the Rule she had sworn to follow; and Bishop John not only deprived John Schoyle of the office of prior of Bruton in 1428 but in the following year sent him to another house of the same Order in Berkshire because he was such a disturbing influence.

Bishop Thomas Bekynton (1443-65) like his predecessors found indiscipline widespread, especially among the Augustinian canons at Keynsham, Taunton and Bruton, and poverty at most of the smaller houses, but no one challenged his authority. His attempt to visit Glastonbury, however, brought him up against Nicholas Frome, who had been abbot there for nearly a quarter of a century when Bekynton arrived. In 1408, when

Archbishop Arundel visited Glastonbury as a result of scandals, Frome had been relieved of his office as almoner and sent to St Augustine's Canterbury. He had returned by 1413 when he was one of the abbey's receivers. By the time of his death in 1455 he was said to have been 100 years old.

Abbot Frome did not much care for the bishop's interference: a visitation was formally begun in the summer of 1445 but its postponement was probably permanent. Correspondence between Frome and Bekynton, at least on the bishop's side, became acrimonious: in the bishop's best style Frome was berated, accused of undue passion with the suggestion that the blindness of his eyes had also affected his brain. There are echoes of the days of Savaric and Jocelin, though Bekynton recognised that his predecessors had lost that battle; but the quarrel involved both archbishops, each acting for the pope, and some of it had degenerated into such questions as whether the abbot should allow church bells to be rung when the bishop passed by. It is more than a little curious that on Easter Monday 1446 the communar at Wells did not give the bearers of St Dunstan's Gift their usual gratuity because they had broken the boxes in which they carried it. In the following year, perhaps inevitably, the bearers did not arrive and the communar paid out 1s 6d in expenses for the subdean and two of the canons to go and fetch it. The gift was last recorded as actually delivered in 1471, but still in 1517 four Glastonbury tenants held their small farms under the obligation of taking the gift to Wells.

Bishop Robert Stillington may or may not have managed to visit Glastonbury; he certainly appointed a commission led by John Alcock, bishop of Rochester, and including two archdeacons and a canon from outside the diocese in July 1472 'in view of the common report that the abbot has been careless and negligent in matters both spiritual and temporal'. There evidently was a problem since at the same time the abbot of Abingdon proposed to make a similar enquiry on behalf of the whole Benedictine congregation in England and appealed to the pope, who compromised, allowing the visit provided both bishop and abbot went together. There seems to have been no trouble when the abbots of St Albans and of Reading proposed visits in 1474 and 1521. Bishop Fox (1492-4) was able to exercise his authority in 1493 when the monks, on the death of Abbot Selwood, held an election for his successor. The abbey's patron, the king, had issued his licence but the bishop had been ignored. Fox thereupon quashed the election and appointed his own candidate, Richard Bere. Fox, keeper of the Privy Seal from 1487, was in little danger of offending Henry VII and the record of his action was carefully noted in his register. The appointment was made on 12 November 1493. A month later Bere, 'nominated as abbot by Episcopal authority, confirmed, instituted and blessed' in the little church of St Aldhelm at Doulting, one of the abbey estates, swore to render canonical obedience to the bishop and his successors. On the next day, pursuant to an order made by the bishop to the archdeacon of Wells, the archdeacon's official installed the new abbot. The bishop's honour was satisfied.

The bishop was, of course, not the only father in God to religious communities. Each head of house stood in that position to all its members; and at least the major Orders developed a system of self-government. The Cluniacs, by their original constitution, deferred to the abbot of Cluny, but when in 1378 the English acknowledged the pope in Rome and the French the pope in Avignon, an English Chapter to govern the Order was set up under two elected abbot presidents. It was not a permanent solution: later, the abbots of Cluny appointed English Cluniacs as their vicars-general; and later still, in 1490, the archbishop of Canterbury became visitor of all Cluniac houses in the country.

The English Cistercians regularly sent representatives to Citeaux as well as keeping up a correspondence with the abbot there but, like the Cluniacs, achieved national independence as a result of the Great Schism. General meetings took place in various convenient towns to deal with discipline, and by the 1430s those meetings were taking place each year at Northampton. Measures taken against relaxation of the Rule were only subject to decision of the General Chapter at Citeaux, conveyed there by two English abbots. Business could still be referred directly to Citeaux, such as the confirmation of the election of Humphrey Quicke, abbot of Cleeve, as the new head of Beaulieu in 1488.

The Benedictines had established a centralised system of government in the early thirteenth century and chapters were held every three years under an abbot president. Northampton was the usual meeting-place by the 1330s and Abbot Chinnock served as president at least three times from 1387. The records of the Benedictines for the fifteenth century are much less full, but Abbot Selwood, staying at Christchurch, Canterbury, in 1465 visited St Augustine's abbey outside the city, whether as abbot president or as a papal judge or commissioner is not known.

The Augustinian chapters, also meeting from the early thirteenth century and often at Northampton or some other midland centre, established a system of local visitation. Thus the prior of Taunton was appointed visitor of the Order's houses in Bath and Wells diocese on seven occasions between 1404 and 1521, the prior of Bruton only once, in 1446. Each house contributed to the visitors' costs: Bruton 26s 8d, Taunton 20s, and Barlinch 6s. Keynsham, affiliated to the Arroasians, was exempted from such oversight until 1521; and the house the Augustinians knew as Brademers, presumably Burtle, was too small to be charged. The heads of the Somerset Augustinian houses occasionally played some official part in the Chapters: the prior of Taunton was involved as an examiner of visitation reports and as auditor of accounts in 1446. At the end of the Chapter held at Leicester in 1509 the priors of Taunton and Plympton were chosen as visitors of the dioceses of Bath and Wells and Exeter and Richard German, a canon of Taunton, was appointed with two others to preach the second Latin sermon. William Yorke, a canon of Bruton, was a preacher in 1518.

In the year 990 Sigeric, bishop of Ramsbury, became archbishop of Canterbury. On the occasion of his appointment Abbot Aelfward of Glastonbury wrote a letter to him which summarised the kind of life expected of the church's leader. Sigeric himself had been a monk at Glastonbury in his youth and now he was urged to take what he had learned in the cloister into the wider world. Humility and generosity were to guide his path, the study of scripture and other suitable books, regular prayer and simplicity of life were to fill his days. This was the view of a monk who saw in the pressures of the world in which the new archbishop had to move something of a threat to his monastic vocation.

The same pressures were felt by any monk who became a bishop and St Hugh regularly returned from his work as bishop of Lincoln to his cell at Witham between his consecration in 1186 and his death in 1200. At least five of the pre-Conquest bishops of Wells had been Glastonbury monks and it may reasonably be assumed that they remained in sympathy with the aims of the religious life while they themselves took on a different role. Robert, formerly a monk of the Cluniac house at Lewes and bishop 1136-66, was the only monastic diocesan bishop in Somerset between the Conquest and the Dissolution, and during his episcopate refused to allow Cistercians to settle in Somerset.

All the other bishops were seculars, more or less personally supportive of the monastic life, but as diocesans bound to exercise jurisdiction as each Order directed or allowed. In practice many of the later bishops relied on suffragans, particularly to ordain clergy, and among them were the Carthusian Richard Viel, the Cluniac Thomas Chard, the Cistercian John Hornse, Augustinian canons John Valens, William Westcarre and William Gilbert, the Carmelite John Bloxwych and the Franciscans John Greenlaw, Thomas Wolf and Francis Sexello. From those suffragans, working as well in Exeter diocese as in Bath and Wells, many Somerset religious received Holy Orders: from fathers in God with particular sympathy for the religious life.

5 What kind of man the abbot ought to be

St Benedict offered an ideal life which, under God, could be achieved through strong and inspired leadership. Monks, he assumed, would sometimes be obstinate, disobedient, proud, murmuring; one or two might habitually transgress the Holy Rule; a few more might be contemptuous of the orders of their seniors. Under a poor leader, discontent and the possibility of scandal were never far away. Leaders and led together came under increasing pressure during the course of the Middle Ages as circumstances brought monasteries closer to the world they had been founded to help men and women leave behind.

The second chapter of St Benedict's Rule lays firmly upon the head of each house the dread responsibility of his position, and it is clear from the history of almost every house that weak leadership led to disaster, but equally that a strong leader could establish a community whose influence might reach far beyond its neighbourhood and might take that very leader far away from his original home.

Among the earliest known heads of houses in Somerset were the first two abbesses of Bath in the seventh century, Berta and Beorngyth, with Folcburg, probably the deputy or prioress. Berta and Folcburg were both Franks, brought to a part of the country where Frankish bishops had ministered for a quarter century. In the tenth century Alfred had to recruit men 'from across the sea' probably from across the Channel in Gaul to live under John the Old Saxon at his new foundation at Athelney and, because he could not find enough to make up the number he wanted, introduced some children, also from Gaul, who were to be trained to be monks later. That was because Viking raids had so devastated the land that religious life had been virtually wiped out.

Few houses anywhere could have had such a head as St Dunstan, abbot of Glastonbury 940 until 957, who established the Benedictine Rule there and whose influence on the monastic life of the whole kingdom was profound. From Glastonbury he moved to become bishop successively of Worcester (957) and London (959) and archbishop of Canterbury (960-88). Of his Saxon successors Aelfstan, formerly a monk of Abingdon, left Glastonbury to be bishop of Ramsbury in 970; Sigar and Brihtwig became bishops of Wells in 975 and 1024 respectively. The last two Saxon abbots, Aethelweard and Aethelnoth, were remembered for having squandered the possessions of the abbey and the latter was deposed in 1077-8 and retired to Canterbury. Most of their successors were remembered as builders, administrators, improvers of the abbey estates, donors of gifts to the abbey church. Perhaps most generous, and certainly most flamboyant of all, was Henry of Blois (abbot 1126-71), who combined the abbacy with the bishopric of Winchester, for a few years (1139-43) was papal legate and played a crucial role in the civil

23 Finely carved capital from the cloister at Glastonbury abbey, dating from the time of Henry of Blois, abbot 1126-71

war between his elder brother Stephen and the Empress Matilda. He has been described as 'the greatest uncanonized English prelate of his century', was a most able financier and administrator, and an unrivalled connoisseur and collector of antiques.

Nicholas Frome, abbot 1420-56, was the chief English delegate at the Council of Basel in 1434, and in the following year was one of the English ambassadors appointed to treat for the reformation of religion and peace with France. Richard Bere, abbot 1493-1524, was also a diplomat, serving as leader of an embassy in Rome in 1504-5, perhaps having been educated in Italy. He was clearly the most distinguished of Glastonbury's later abbots: esteemed by the Renaissance humanist Erasmus, who praised his liberality towards scholars, among whom was Richard Pace, Cardinal Wolsey's faithful diplomat. A contemporary was a little more reticent: 'good, honest, virtuous, wise and discrete as well as a grave man'. Among members of his household were a French poet, a harper and an 'arasman', presumably a specialist in making woven hangings or tapestries.

The other Somerset monasteries after the Conquest were not so fortunate in their leaders, though Hugh of Avalon clearly proved himself a giant among men. St Hugh came to Witham from Burgundy highly recommended and his personal qualities, which brought such success to Witham, led to his appointment as bishop of Lincoln (1186-1200). John of Somerton, abbot of Muchelney 1334-47, was evidently a personal friend of Bishop Ralph of Shrewsbury. Most of his contemporaries were the objects of the bishop's severe criticism for the indiscipline of their houses.

In the later fifteenth century Bruton produced William Gilbert (1495-1532), an Oxford graduate in theology, through whose exertions the status of the house was elevated from priory to abbey and himself from prior to abbot. Gilbert, who was one of the parties to the foundation of a grammar school at Bruton, was in 1519 consecrated bishop of a see which in its shortened Latin form appears as *Majoren*, probably a place in the Middle East from which Christians had long been driven by Muslims. The empty title allowed him to be employed by bishops in England in need of help, and he thus found himself ordaining clergy for the absent bishops of Bath and Wells, Exeter and Winchester. Such a position also permitted him, for instance, to be appointed in 1525 vicar of South Petherton.

Appointment as suffragan bishop certainly implied influence beyond the confines of the cloister but not necessarily the kind of spiritual depth of a Dunstan or a Hugh. Richard Viel, a remarkably young prior of Witham by 1447, left his cell without leave and an order for his arrest was issued. He was clearly a man of influence for he was an executor of the great Cardinal Beaufort: no wonder he was reinstated for a time, but he evidently resigned in 1458 and was made bishop of Killala in Ireland in the following year. After that, with no possibility of being pastor of his wild western Irish flock, he lived the life of a secular priest, serving as suffragan to the bishop of Bath and Wells in 1465.

John Valens, a former Augustinian canon from Suffolk, was made bishop of Tenos in 1459 and served as suffragan for 20 years, probably living from 1462 at Wells as master of St John's hospital. He was followed both as suffragan and master by Thomas Cornish, a member of the Order of St John of Jerusalem, who served in Bath and Wells diocese until his death in 1513 and in Exeter diocese until 1505. And after him both William Gilbert and Thomas Chard served as suffragan, the latter prior of Montacute from 1514 until 1532 when he retired to Montacute's cell at Carswell in Devon. Chard had been consecrated bishop of Selymbria in 1508.

There were a few men distinguished in other ways in the years just before the Dissolution. Among them was Edmund Horde, formerly a skilful lawyer in Oxford, who became a Carthusian monk in London and was appointed prior of Hinton by 1529. Only the persuasion of his brother, also a lawyer, prevented him from defying the royal officers when they came to dissolve his house in 1539. In his will he left a book to the monastery of Sheen 'if it should be re-edified'. Another man of distinction was the last prior of Montacute, Robert Whitlocke, Gybbes or Shirborne. At the Dissolution in 1539 he was awarded a large pension and a house in East Chinnock. Just over 20 years later in his will he mentioned a 'lymbeck', that is an alembic, a vessel used for distilling alcohol, three 'stillatories', a brass pot 'to make *aqua vita* in', 20 dozen glasses, and books of physic and surgery. Evidently he practised medicine; but so many glasses suggest his alcohol might also have been for social consumption. William Holloway, the last prior of Bath, was also a scientist: he apparently used the hot waters of his city instead of fire in his experiments.

But abbots and priors were not universally successful nor inspiring. John the Old Saxon, chosen by King Alfred for the new foundation at Athelney, came, as his name implies, from beyond the North Sea and presumably had a reputation which attracted the king. Attempts on his life suggest his popularity was not universal. Thurstan was deposed from Glastonbury by William I for his insensitive treatment of his monks, and Abbot Robert was ejected from Muchelney in 1191. Two prioresses of Barrow seem to have been

24 William Whete, fomer prior of Stavordale, found to have been killed by a forester, 1391

forced to resign for incompetence, but were at least allowed to stay in their house. Removal from office as head of a religious house was by no means uncommon.

Distinguished leaders naturally attracted and produced in their turn men of quality, and the influence of St Dunstan spread across southern England as monks of Glastonbury were promoted: St Aethelwold to be the first abbot of Abingdon *c*.954 and bishop of Winchester 963; Sigeric to be abbot of St Augustine's, Canterbury, *c*.980, bishop of Ramsbury 985, archbishop of Canterbury 990; Aelfmar and Lyfing via Tavistock to be respectively bishop of Selsey in 1009 and of Worcester 1027; and Aethelgar from Glastonbury to Abingdon, then abbot of New Minster 964, bishop of Selsey 980 and archbishop of Canterbury 988.

No other house in the county has such a record either then or later. Indeed, there was, on the whole after the Conquest, much less movement between houses in terms of promotion either to be bishop or to be head of another house. There were, of course, exceptions, such as Simon Crassus, who came to be abbot of Athelney from Abingdon *c*.1136; Master Walter, formerly sub-prior of Hyde, who became prior of Bath in the 1190s; or the Norman Clarembaud, prior of Montacute until *c*.1158, who moved on to be prior of Thetford and for ten years from 1163 was abbot of St Augustine's, Canterbury. Later still, until the 1530s, such moves were rare, especially between orders, and the transfers of the Benedictine Robert Newton from Glastonbury to be prior of the Cluniac Montacute in 1458 or of Prior John Dunster of Bath to be abbot of St Augustine's, Canterbury, were unusual. The prior and convent of Beaulieu elected Cleeve's abbot, Humphrey Quicke, in 1488 because of his learning and devotion to religion, but the transfers of Robert Hamlyn in 1533 from Tavistock to Athelney and of Henry Man in 1534 from Sheen to Witham were moves by Cardinal Wolsey to place amenable men in positions of authority.

6 Men and women like any other

Heads of houses whose names have survived represent only a small proportion of the men and women who devoted themselves, for better or worse, to the religious life. Their lesser brothers and sisters are much more elusive, yet it is important to discover something about the origins, social standing and activities of as many as possible in order to understand why the religious life was attractive to them.

Origins

Perhaps it was an exaggeration by Alfred's biographer to emphasise the great work of revival the king achieved that details of the foreign origins of the first monks of Athelney were recorded. The evidence from Glastonbury, however, suggests that the community there at least in the early tenth century may have been Irish. By the time of the Conquest the monks were Saxon through and through as Abbot Thurstan found to his cost.

The first monks at Montacute came from Cluny or from another house of the Order in England, and it was Cluniac policy to fill vacancies quickly. So between March 1297 and August 1304 five monks died, beginning with Prior Geoffrey de Dosa, evidently not English, and followed by two local men John of Wells and Henry of Sherborne and two others. They were replaced immediately by order of the abbot of Cluny so that the services of the church might be duly performed. The first monks of Cleeve almost certainly came from the founding house at Revesby in Lincolnshire.

Several of the early members of the Charterhouse at Witham are known by name and background. Norbert and a small group of monks first came over from Burgundy c.1178-9. Also at Witham then or soon after were Bovo, Aimard and Gerard, all from Burgundy. Perhaps surprisingly in view of its difficult start, Witham soon became popular with Englishmen: among the first recruits were Robert FitzHenry and Ralph from St Swithun's, Winchester, and Adam from Dryburgh abbey in Scotland. Others from Bath and Muchelney came for a while but left for different reasons.

At about the same time as the first recruits were going to Witham, it was decided that the sisters of the Order of St John of Jerusalem should be brought together from houses all over England to what came to be called Minchin Buckland — two from Hertfordshire, one from Norfolk, two from Cambridgeshire, one from Buckinghamshire and two from Oxfordshire.

From the earlier thirteenth century most if not all the abbots of Glastonbury were already monks there, with surnames such as Amesbury, Petherton, Taunton, Sodbury, Chinnock, Frome and Selwood suggesting origins not far away. Abbots John of Kent, John of Breinton (Herefordshire) and Walter of Monington (Pembrokeshire) were drawn to Glastonbury from a much greater distance. In the later Middle Ages the clues to origins are a little more obvious. Among the community in 1408, for instance, were men whose names suggest where they came from, most within a few miles of the abbey but only two actually from its own estates: Bodmin, Crewkerne, Muchelney, Taunton, Draycott, Gloucester, Knowle, Pedwell, Stanton, Bristol, Camel, Barrington, Frome, Moorlinch, Langport, Mudford and Bradford.

A similar story is told at Keynsham in 1377 when there were two canons bearing the name Keynsham and others who probably came from Newton, Berkeley, Marshfield, Chew and Farleigh. A century later monks of Bath were named from Dunster, Lacock, Abingdon, Keynsham, Salisbury, Bath, Bristol, Framilode, Chew, Pensford and Swainswick, and in 1496 from Pensford, Norton, Abingdon, Swainswick, Widcombe, Bristol, Bath, Wick, Worcester, Keynsham and Beckington.

Canons at Bruton bore surnames which included Oxford, Wilton, Backwell, Alford, Wells, Yatton and Dunster. John Lamprey is known to have come from Wells, John Henton from Bruton and William Gilbert from nearby Whitcombe in Corton Denham. Two of the last four priors of Hinton were remembered as local: John Taylor *alias* Chamberlain had been born in Chamberlain Street, Wells, and Henry Corsley in Frome.

In striking contrast to such localisation and the stability which was the tradition especially of the Benedictines, the friars were almost by nature travellers, staying a few years in one house and then moving on. For that reason among others their numbers are rarely known, their names ill-recorded. Bridgwater's friars were often connected with their house at Oxford, from which several of their learned and distinguished wardens came, and at least seven during the fifteenth century were foreigners: Louis de Colonia, Theodoric Wellinc, Reynold Gronigh, John de Stauria, James Schruade, Peter de Subenicho and Conrad Doliatoris.

Social background

The monks at Glastonbury in 1377 included only two whose names obviously indicate gentle birth, William la Zouche and Thomas FitzJames. William's family paid him a pension of 10 marks (£6 13s 4d) a year between 1361 and 1390 from the family estates. Three monks there in the fifteenth century received special privileges from the pope and had to reveal their vital details: Hugh Foster was 'of noble birth' and John West was described both as 'of a noble race of barons' and as son of an unmarried noble, a baron, and an unmarried woman. He was probably son of Reginald West, Lord de la Warr. John Brygge was the illegitimate son of a married man and an unmarried woman, but presumably not so noble. John Benett's father was in trade, but respectable enough, for Thomas Eloyet was a burgess of Bristol. The many surnames deriving from towns or villages of origin suggest more modest backgrounds, many recruits coming from the abbey's own estates. They were, perhaps, more likely to have been men from the countryside.

There were a few gentlefolk in other houses, such as the 21-year-old canon of Bruton who in 1273 was declared to be the heir to the lands of his late parents Richard and Anastasia Wason. Whether he was faithful to his vows or returned to the world in face of such temptation is not known. Another was Hugh Boscawen of Witham, ordained deacon at Fisherton in Wiltshire in 1447. Witham was the nearest Carthusian house to his home in Cornwall. Families like Boscawen's found nunneries suitable places for unmarriageable daughters and sisters as well as finishing schools for those with prospects and places where heiresses might be placed to divert their property to grasping hands.

Among the 50 sisters at Minchin Buckland in 1232 was Agnes, daughter of the earl of Arundel; and in 1311 Isabel, daughter of Thomas of Berkeley, was living there, supported by an annual rent of £4 from one of her father's estates. Thomas Woth, not at all in the same social class, saw Cannington as a suitable home for his about-to-be-orphaned daughter in 1407 leaving the prioress forty marks (£26 13s 4d) to keep her up to the age of ten years and a further eleven marks (£7 6s 8d) to provide a dowry on her marriage. Elizabeth Hull was at Buckland in 1416 when her mother died, leaving her a large sum in cash, a silver-gilt cup and cover, and a set of coral beads. The Verney family of Fairfield in Stogursey included Cecily, the last prioress of Cannington and her niece Joan, who was a member of the community at Buckland at the Dissolution.

A court case in 1383 revealed a situation rich in dramatic possibilities. David Cervington brought

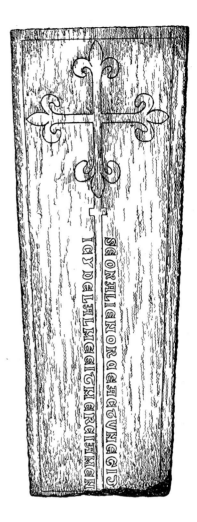

25 Incised slab commemorating Eleanor of Actune, sister at Minchin Buckland about 1300

a claim before the bishop of Bath and Wells' court declaring that Clarice Stil, then not quite eight years old, had been taken to Buckland and placed in the care of two sisters there who told her that if she passed out of the priory door 'the devil would carry her away'. David claimed that in practice she had been abducted by one Walter Reynold and with the connivance of the prioress of Buckland, so that Clarice would be disinherited in favour of Walter's wife. Not so, answered Walter: there was no such plan; only that she should stay for two years 'to see if the life would please her'. But two years later, still only aged ten, she assumed the religious habit. That last was a fact, however much she was influenced unduly. David Cervington lost the case.

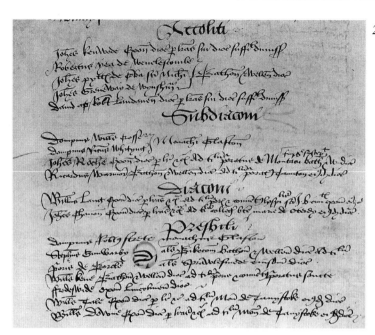

26 Richard Whiting becomes a sub-deacon, 22 December 1498

By the end of the Middle Ages the religious life was attracting members of the rising merchant class. John Henton, prior of Bruton 1448-95, was the son of a prosperous businessman in the town. His successor William Gilbert was of yeoman stock. William Brymmer was probably son of John and Alice Brymmer who owned a large farm in Bruton parish, and Richard Bogye, the last prior, was stepson to John Tyler, a Wells clothmaker.

Apart from the Verneys of Fairfield, two other genteel families seem to have contributed more than their share of religious. Richard Whiting, the last abbot of Glastonbury, came from the Wrington area. A Thomas Whiting had been a monk at Glastonbury in the later fourteenth century and until after 1408, a John Whiting in 1492. Another Richard Whiting, probably the abbot's uncle, was chamberlain at Bath, a relative was later a nun at Wilton, and two nieces after the death of their uncle went abroad and became nuns in Bruges. Likewise the Hadleys of Withycombe: James Hadley was a pious and prosperous esquire who wanted his sons brought up in the law, perhaps as a reaction to the rest of his immediate family. His brother John was a canon of Bruton, brother William was a canon at Barlinch and brother Henry was a secular priest. James mentioned them all in his will which he drew up in 1532. William Hadley was among those canons who surrendered Barlinch in 1536 but there is no John Hadley among the canons of Bruton pensioned in 1539. He is there, however, under the name John Dunster, a place far better known to Bruton than the tiny village of his birth.

Finally, two Carthusians came from what might be called the intellectual elite. John Blacman of Witham was a Somerset man and a scholar of repute whose career in the secular world brought him to the notice of King Henry VI. He had been a fellow of Merton College, Oxford, then successively fellow and precentor of Eton and warden of King's Hall, Cambridge, both institutions close to the heart of the king. From there he moved to a parish and then to the deanery of the college of Westbury on Trym near Bristol. About 1459 he resigned and became a member of the community at Witham. Edmund Horde of Hinton was also an Oxford man, a fellow of All Souls college for 15 years and a distinguished lawyer. In 1520 he gave up his legal practice and three livings and seems to have become a Carthusian in London before becoming prior of Hinton.

Aspiring to perfection

Dunstan and Hugh, two of Somerset's few saints, were recognised as such not as a result of pressure from kings nor the decisions of popes, but almost by popular acclamation very soon after their respective deaths. They may stand as models for local religious to emulate. Adam of Dryburgh, attracted to Hugh and to the strict life of Witham from his home north of the border, produced from the depth of his spirituality books entitled *Soliloquy on the Instruction of the Soul*, *On the Fourfold Discipline of the Cell*, *The Mirror of Discipline* and *My Own Secret* which came to be used and studied widely within his Order. Later in the Middle Ages Witham also attracted John Blacman, and Hinton became home to the saintly John Luscote, prior in 1394, as well as Edmund Horde.

Among the Franciscan friars of Bridgwater only a very few names are even known, but quite a large proportion were men of learning and piety. Among them were two Oxford theologians Henry Cross and William Auger, the latter the author of a commentary on St Luke's gospel. Other houses may have welcomed saints unaware. Thomas Lemyngton asked in 1398 to be transferred from Winchester to Glastonbury 'for the sake of a stricter regular discipline'. Sixty years later Robert Newton, a monk of Glastonbury, was elected prior of Montacute but resigned in 1462 and remained in the much poorer, stricter and no doubt much less comfortable house for another 30 years.

In such close and sometimes intense communities enthusiasm might break out. Hinton at the end of the fifteenth century produced two examples. Brother Stephen, also known as 'the admirable Stephen', experienced visions of St Mary Magdalene and a dream of being transported to the top of a mountain where in a beautiful garden he prostrated himself before a lady of extreme beauty who called him 'lover'. A year or two later Nicholas Hopkins no doubt embarrassed his Order by uttering cryptic prophecies, especially for the ears of Edward Stafford, duke of Buckingham. What he told the duke was heard to be treasonable and while Buckingham was executed Hopkins was removed to the Tower and probably later to some other Charterhouse. He was the 'Chartreux friar . . . that devil-monk' immortalised by Shakespeare in *Henry VIII*.

An atmosphere of spiritual endeavour is perhaps the best that can be claimed for communities producing such men, but they still could inspire by prayer and by example. Edmund Leversedge, a young man from Frome, had a vision of Purgatory. His record of the experience ends with a reference to his 'frend of Wytham', one of the brethren there who had inspired him.

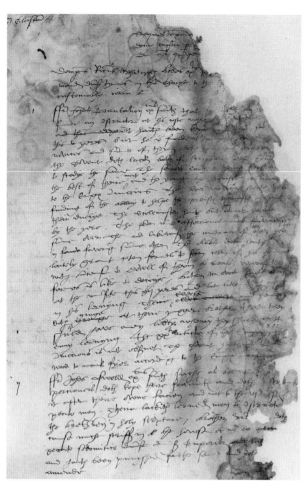

27 Glastonbury abbey is visited, 1538

Ill-suited to the Religious life

The Rule of St Benedict demanded, and still demands, a great deal of those who try to live by it. Any closed community which is not well led and inspired will give opportunities for petty jealousies and ambitions; the call of the world, never far away, often proved attractive, and a lax régime could expose the most vulnerable. On the whole the houses of Augustinian canons, always much less strict in their approach to the outside world, found themselves more severely criticised by visiting bishops. The Carthusians and other strict Orders were clearly more successful and in the years immediately before the Dissolution proved to be both attractive to recruits and centres of popular devotion.

But in every community there were tensions. St Benedict wrote of deans with positions of responsibility, of seniors and younger monks, of boys and adolescents; all members of the community but with a built-in generation gap. Perhaps inevitably, given the size of some communities and the complexity of administration entailed, the gifts and personalities of individuals made them prominent and gradually privileged and left others feeling they were undervalued. When in July 1538 Bishop John Clerke visited

Glastonbury, Martin Indract claimed that younger brethren held offices but were not as assiduous in their duties 'as the old men doth', John Selwood reported that there was no charity among the young towards the old and John Pantaleon said 'elders and seniors doth grudge at their yonger brethren'. The emphasis on seniority, an acknowledgement of stability and order, had become a rock of offence.

Privilege of office and seniority inevitably led to personal desire for promotion. Thomas Coffyn, perhaps the best-educated monk of Glastonbury of his time, bemoaned his failure to be elected abbot of Glastonbury in 1375. Without the new abbot's permission he took his case to Rome and was therefore declared an apostate. Some kind of settlement must have been made between him and his rival, but he was still making a nuisance of himself in 1408. Two others seeking promotion, both from Bruton, were William Hows, who in 1482 obtained from the pope a dispensation that he might be promoted despite blindness in one eye; and Richard Thomlyn, who wrote quite openly to Thomas Cromwell in 1528 asking him to persuade Wolsey to request the abbacy of Bristol for himself.

Much more common, from before the middle of the fourteenth century, were monks who sought from the pope the kind of spiritual benefits which men outside community were prepared to give money for. The rights to choose a confessor or to receive plenary remission at the time of death were obtained by several monks from Glastonbury, and no doubt from other Somerset houses. Others were similarly privileged to hear mass before daybreak, to accept secular benefices even with cure, or to hold office as papal chaplains. Senior monks on retiring from office were sometimes permitted to retain their rooms and extra allowances of food and drink for their lives. The idea of community, of common arrangements for eating and sleeping, the antithesis of privilege, had long since disappeared.

In 1408 Baldwin Rosemond, a member of the Glastonbury community, was reported to have obtained bulls from the pope for exemptions and licence to have privileges and to hold benefices. He denied the accusation, but at the time he could have pointed to a long tradition there that monks had obtained privileges of the same kind.

The experience of Hugh Foster, also of Glastonbury, was unusual only in its survival. In 1434 he received papal permission to choose his confessor. Twelve years later, after a long period away from the house at Oxford where he graduated a bachelor in canon law and was made a papal chaplain, he received a further appointment as a penitentiary in St Peter's in Rome and in the Roman court. Five years later he evidently had a change of heart but needed the pope's support to get back home, 'to have his accustomed place in chapter and choir' as he had 'no intention of giving up regular observance'. But still, equality was not quite what he sought for and, described as 'of noble birth', he received a dispensation to hold a secular benefice.

There was privilege of birth and privilege of office. Office brought with it obvious responsibilities. Thomas Arundel, archbishop of Canterbury, visited Glastonbury in 1408 at the instigation of the king and the request of Abbot Chinnock. The community was rife with bitterness and dissension, caused in no small part because the abbot had chosen for office men who were said to be immature, weak-minded, improvident and dishonest. The archbishop's judgement was to remove the two cellarers, the almoner, the sub-prior, the third prior, the hosteller, the chamberlain, the kitchen steward and the prior's chaplain and to pension off the prior, none other than the learned Thomas Coffyn. Further, three of those were sent to other monasteries, two were imprisoned within the abbey and three were sent back to the cloister to work and pray unburdened by outside duties.

Clearly for some the decision to enter a monastery was a dreadful mistake, and in many cases there was little sympathy for the backslider. John de Worthy, a monk at Muchelney in 1338, was sentenced on account of his disobedience to live in a single room on a restricted diet; his brethren were later criticised for showing sympathy for his plight. In 1355 Henry de Lyle, head of the tiny house at Horsley in Gloucestershire, but answerable to the prior of Bruton, was accused of wasteful expenditure by the prior. Instead of facing the charge he went to Rome and Venice without the permission of his superior and proved the accusation true by spending the enormous sum of £60. Two years later he was said to have renounced his vow and in 1358 was deposed. William Cary was another Bruton canon described as a wanderer (vagabond) in the 1370s, and in the 1440s the bishop was told of two more Bruton canons, John Lamyet and John Pawle, who had 'long ago' left the priory.

Robert Bowrman and Philip Fylle both left Athelney in 1512 and were said by Abbot Wellyngton to be wandering abroad to the peril of their souls. Thomas Ansell, also of Athelney, declared to the visiting bishop:

> that he was put owt of the religion by the king's visitors and restored againe againste his will by his friends. And the Abbot doth kepe hym in religion against his wil. Ande wold be owt again if he can.

By contrast there were a few whose fears or ambitions had consequences which overwhelmed them. John of Nunney left Glastonbury for Eynsham but after six months found himself embroiled in a dispute between rival candidates for the abbacy which he could not handle and in 1345 needed permission to return. William Estrete, another from Glastonbury, went to Rome with his abbot's consent for the Jubilee Indulgence and for some private legal business. He evidently lost his case and was imprisoned, but taking advantage of a prison break returned home. His abbot took the strict view: he had been justly imprisoned and had incurred the sentence of excommunication for escaping; he could not, therefore, be admitted to Glastonbury. In 1451 William persuaded the pope to order the abbot to absolve him and take him back.

The unseemly quarrel between John Dunster and John Cantlow during the period 1483-7 illustrates well many aspects of the monastic life in the century before the Dissolution. The rather fragmentary papers relating to the quarrel, which seems to have been heard at the end of the period in the new court of Star Chamber, tell only a small part of the story and the outcome is quite unknown, but it is clear that the two men, both attempting to follow the Rule of St Benedict, found themselves, both during the quarrel and after it, not entirely the exemplars that the head of a house ought to be.

Dunster, it emerges, was a native of Bath. He evidently belonged to one of the mercantile families of the city, for his mother was Alice Slougge, presumably related in some way to John Slogye, who held a tenement of the mayor and commonalty in Walcot street in the city in 1475 and of John Slugg, one of the city constables in 1497. The name Dunster was presumably adopted when he entered Bath's cell at Dunster. He returned to the mother house in or before 1481 when he is referred to as prior. In the following year he was elected abbot of St Augustine's, Canterbury, where he ruled until his death in 1496.

It is particularly ironic that Cantlow should have accused Dunster of misappropriation and profligate spending since Dunster was already being officially spoken of as the king's candidate to replace the incompetent Abbot Sellyng at Canterbury in the summer of 1480 when Sellyng was being threatened with excommunication on the orders of the pope. The appointment was evidently of international concern since St Augustine's was 'immediately subject to the church of Rome' but the king insisted on the appointment of his own nominee. No action had evidently been taken against Sellyng in 1480 but by early July 1482 he had resigned and later in the month the king signified to Pope Sixtus that he assented to Dunster's election. Four months later the pope formally approved, but not until March 1483 was Dunster allowed to enjoy the income of his new office. The move from Bath to Canterbury had evidently been very costly.

7 The world at the gates

Charity

'In the reception of the poor . . . the greatest care and solicitude should be shown'. St Benedict had decreed that hospitality should be offered to those who asked for it, and Abbot Herluin, the second Norman abbot of Glastonbury, threatened to have the abbey porter's ears cut off if he refused to allow the poor to enter the abbey. In 1451 Bishop Bekynton, in the same spirit, reminded the canons of Keynsham that those eating in the refectory were to put aside a part of their helpings for the common alms. The bishop felt the need to remind them again in 1455 with the threat of loss of half the next meal. The same bishop after visiting Muchelney ordered that houses near the north gate of the abbey 'anciently founded and ordained for the maintenance of poor persons out of the alms of the abbot and convent' should be rebuilt either on the same site or a more suitable place 'to the end that poor persons may from henceforth be maintained as of old'.

The commissioners acting for the government of Henry VIII in the great inquiry into monastic finances in 1535 were not particularly interested in what was given away. They recorded only alms in cash distributed in the name of founders and patrons as an allowable item against the gross income of each monastery. So they recorded only £6 13s 4d which Muchelney was to give in the name of its royal founders. Athelney's royal donations totalled £22 2s out of a total of £27 8s 8d. Bath was supposed to give away rather less than Muchelney to 'divers poor and leprous' people. Montacute should have spent over £21 on seven paupers in commemoration of the soul of the count of Mortain, 13s 4d to remember King John, and 34s 4d for Richard Chitterne and his parents making a total of £23 8s 7½d. Taunton's total of £32 5s 8d was not quite as generous as it appears, because it included the alms given by its affiliated house of Stavordale. Taunton was supposed to give away 3s 4d every Friday according to the ordinance of its first (though chronologically second) founder, Henry of Blois, Bishop of Winchester, and 14d every Sunday by gift of William Giffard, its second founder, and 34s to seven paupers from founders unnamed. Four paupers were to be given a total of £12 4s a year at Stavordale and a further sum of 53s 4d.

Those sums were very small: Bath was apparently offering £10 2s 6d in alms out of a total gross income of over £695; Keynsham £10 15s out of £417. We shall never know the whole truth, because annual accounts from neither Bath nor Keynsham have survived to show what other sums might have been given away, but a closer look at some fourteenth-century endowments at Glastonbury and some accounts for 1538-9 suggest a much greater generosity.

Thus the celebration of John of Kent's obit founded in 1303 included gifts of £1 0s 5d worth of bread for the poor distributed on John's anniversary and on the feast of the Translation of St Thomas of Canterbury. Abbot Adam of Sodbury's endowment for his family and for Prior John of Breinton included bread doles three times a year.

The king's accountants in 1535 recorded that alms given by the monks of Glastonbury were worth £155 16s 8d, which included £5 for the support of 10 poor widows in what came to be known as Abbot Bere's almshouses. The surviving accounts for 1538-9 tell a very different story. In that year the prior accounted for the cost of the widows in the almshouse, providing each with two meals a day and two waggonloads of fuel. The almoner provided food, clothing and shrouds for poor people and his deputy gave them 10 quarters of beans on the eve of the feast of St Patrick. The 'Almoner's House' comprised three rooms and a buttery and the under-Almoner had both a room for himself and a bakehouse to produce the bread for all who presented themselves at the door. In the same year the keeper of the anniversary fund of Abbot Monington produced 32s worth of corn, presumably for the bread. Accounts from other departments within the abbey have not survived and whether the total amounted to over £155 is not possible to say. Earlier accounts recorded similar payments: six quarters and six bushels of wheat from the foreign cellarer in 1529-30 to remember the late Abbot Bere; 48s for four quarters of frumenty for bread for the poor, also from Monington's keeper; small payments made by the chamberlain in 1307-8 and 1309-10. Other gifts made directly to the poor on each of the abbey's estates might easily have been made, and it is fair to assume that the poor and beggars received the remnants of the monastery supper table as they did at Keynsham.

Glastonbury was prosperous. Much less well off was Montacute, which in 1538-9 actually admitted to giving away only 53s 4d. But in that year the priory made an operating loss of over £32 and something had to go.

The accounts of 1535 might, of course, have been designed to hide more than they revealed, but the evidence of visitations suggests that enthusiasm for giving money away was not great. The brethren at Athelney in 1538 said they lacked an almoner to distribute their fragments, that is food left over from their meals. Those at Glastonbury complained in the same year that no house was provided for poor wayfaring men and fragments were deliberately thrown away. The closure of Cleeve in 1536 produced much dismay in the neighbourhood and the supply of 53 sheep and an ox for the household there in its last months suggests that the reported 'lamentations' were justified. Such generosity was in addition to the £12 13s 8d in alms the abbey admitted distributing for the souls of Hugh Luttrell, John Sydenham and others.

Hospitals

Care for the poor, sick and aged as enjoined in the Gospels was the specific concern of a small number of what were usually known as hospitals which appeared from the late eleventh century onwards. They were usually in or near towns — Bath, Bedminster and Redcliffe near Bristol, Bridgwater, Bruton, Glastonbury, Ilchester, Langport, Taunton and Wells. Most were not in the strict sense monastic foundations, but at least some of them were administered by people living a community life, and those still operating in that way at the Dissolution were dissolved. Most, however, had changed their system of government and remained, often as almshouses.

Details of the work of hospitals have survived badly: only the foundation deed of one has been preserved to give some idea of the kind of care offered and of its limitations. William Brewer, founder of St John's hospital at Bridgwater before 1213, intended a community for the care of 13 infirm people and for the shelter of pilgrims and religious passing through the town. In 1219 Bishop Jocelin seems to have redefined its purpose as 'a free, pure and perpetual *Domus Dei* for Christ's poor only', and the definition of poor was carefully prescribed:

> no lepers, lunatics, or persons having the falling sickness or other contagious disease, and no pregnant women or sucking infants, and no intolerable persons, even though they be poor and infirm.

If any should be admitted by mistake they were to be expelled as soon as possible, and other recovered patients were 'to be let out without delay'. No numbers were specified, but care staff 'to be watchful and ready night and day, to help the infirm and to minister to them in all things' were limited to two or three women. Those rules, incidentally, were still in operation in 1457 and no criticism of the hospital was apparently made after a visitation in 1463.

The community at Bridgwater hospital originally comprised a master or prior and 'some' brethren. Bishop Jocelin added the two or three women and Bishop Robert Burnell in 1298 established a community of a master and 13 brothers, and in addition 13 poor scholars. By 1539, when the hospital was dissolved, there were a master and seven brethren. St John's at Bath began in 1180 and in 1260 was also a religious community under a master and comprising brothers and sisters. Only brothers were there by the 1330s and by 1535 there was only a master; the hospital was thus not considered a religious community and was not dissolved.

A similar distinction was made at other hospitals. St John's at Wells, founded by the brothers Hugh and Jocelin of Wells, was always financially unstable and the number of brothers varied. In 1350 it was hoped to increase the community to a prior and ten brothers but there were only two in 1439 and 1445, five in 1462, and the prior and three were pensioned in 1539. The hospital of the Holy Trinity at Whitehall, Ilchester, founded by 1220, was certainly a religious community in the 1240s, having both men and women, though by 1281 it seems to have been an exclusively female one and to have ceased to be a hospital. The nuns had left by 1463.

The other hospitals survived dissolution because by that date they had ceased to be religious communities. St Katherine's at Bedminster had 'several' brethren at its foundation in the early thirteenth century; in the early fifteenth century a warden and from two to four priests; and in the 1530s only one priest, the master. The hospital of St Katherine at Lusty outside Bruton, founded by 1291, had a master or warden and *confratres* in 1532, but they were probably lay supporters rather than resident brothers. St John's in Redcliffe outside Bristol was run by brothers and sisters at its foundation in the early

28 Licence to collect money for Bruton hospital, 1532

thirteenth century but soon had men only, and in 1442 only one brother. The foundation had thus become a single cure and as such was dissolved in 1544. A master and brethren comprised the community on the outskirts of Taunton by 1236. By 1307 one of the canons of Taunton priory was employed to take services in the chapel and minister to the sick but the hospital was actually in the care of a group of lay people under a master chosen by the canon. The hospital of St John at Glastonbury, financed at first by the abbey almoner, was removed to a new site and independent governance *c*.1250 and nearly disappeared in 1548 when it was thought to have been a chantry.

Little has survived to allow reconstruction of the work of these institutions, but their purpose is usually clear. The hospitals at Bath were presumably for the sick and poor visiting the city for the waters as well as for natives; St John's was later said to have been for six poor men. Bedminster was for the sick and infirm and for the needy traveller, Ilchester for poor travellers and pilgrims rather than sick. Specifically, hospitals at Bruton, Ilchester, Langport and Taunton were at times said to have been for lepers. Taunton alone apart from Bridgwater yields some clue to administration: 6d was to be paid on entry to the house and 6d for burial.

1 *Christot as Wisdom with St Dunstan at his feet; from 'St Dunstan's Classbook'*

2 *Brent Knoll, according to legend the gift of King Arthur to Glastonbury abbey*

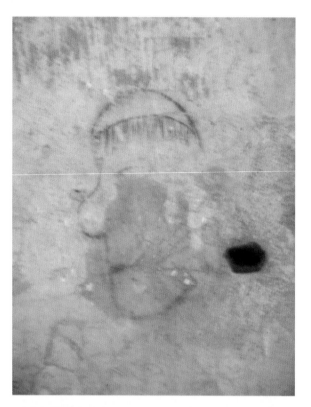

3 Cleeve abbey: a rare portrait on
a passage wall in the south range

4 The tower of the chapel of St Michael on Glastonbury Tor

5 *Bath abbey (cathedral priory), the inspiration of Bishop Oliver King and the work of Robert and William Vertue*

6   *Banners at rest during Evensong: Glastonbury Pilgrimage 1989*

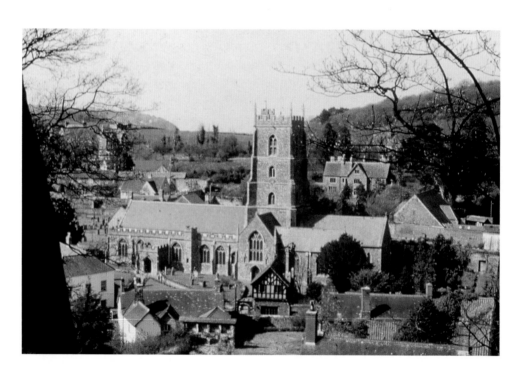

7   *The priory and parish church of Dunster from the castle mound*

8   *Cleeve abbey dormitory. Traces of partition walls show the compromise between community and privacy*

9   *St Dunstan and the devil in stained glass*

10 St Mary Magdalene's hospital, Glastonbury. The surviving north range and chapel

11 Burrow Mump and its eighteenth-century unfinished chapel. An outpost of Athelney by the Parrett, an earlier chapel perhaps a guide to river traffic

12 *Remote Woodspring priory. Crossing tower and nave of church and nearby barn preserved as the centre of a farm*

13 *The great fishpool at Emborough, leased to the Carthusians of Hinton from 1524 but virtually emptied of fish and water in 1532 by aggressive locals*

14 *Court Barn, West Bradley: early fifteenth-century storage for tithes paid to Glastonbury's rectory*

15 *Cleeve abbey gatehouse, built in the thirteenth century and remodelled by Abbot William Dovell (1507-36)*

16 Mells: the courtyard of the Talbot inn, part of a new street built by Abbot John Selwood of Glastonbury about 1470

17 A late-medieval shop in High Street, Glastonbury, often and wrongly called the Tribunal

18 *The dovecot, Dunster priory. It contains 540 nesting boxes*

19 *The parish church, Witham Friary, formerly the chapel of the Carthusian lay brothers*

20 *The Lady Chapel, Glastonbury abbey, begun soon after the great fire of 1184 on the site of the earliest churches*

21 St Michael's tower, Glastonbury Tor, after a Spring shower. Tower and Tor are a symbol of both power and tragedy

22 Montacute Borough, 1848. A borough was part of the priory's original endowment about 1102 and its extension by two priors included a market place and two streets

23 Cleeve abbey, the refectory roof in the south range, built by Abbot William Dovell (1507-36)

24 The crypt at Muchelney, perhaps of the eighth century

25 *The site (behind trees) of Minchin Buckland priory and preceptory, at the eastern edge of Durston village*

26 *Meare, the abbot of Glastonbury's fish house, built by 1313 but much altered and restored. The mere behind was up to five miles in circumference*

27 Cannington priory. The parish church stands in places almost touching Cannington Court, which still contains much of the fabric of the medieval nunnery

28 Bath, Holloway Chapel: the chapel of St Mary Magdalene's hospital built by Prior John Cantlow in 1495 and enlarged in the early nineteenth century

29 *Taunton, Priory Barn, 1909. In fact a range adjoining a gateway between the priory buildings and the meadows, including re-used architectural details of the thirteenth century and later*

30 *Woodspring priory from the air. Cloister, sacristy, chapter house and infirmary have been excavated and identified*

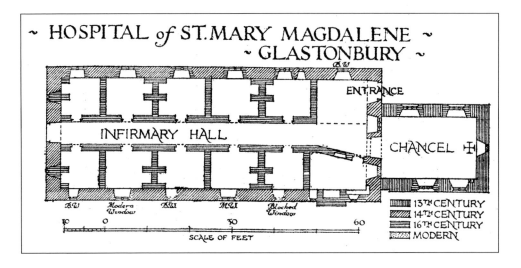

29 Plan of St Mary Magdalene's hospital, Glastonbury

Pressures on purses

Thanks to founders' generosity, monasteries and a few hospitals became landowners and capitalists, some of them very substantial, ranking with the great lay owners. The abbot of Glastonbury and the prior of Bath sat in Parliament; most religious houses, save the very poorest, paid taxes like parish clergy. Many became assets to founders and powerful neighbours, and especially to successive kings, retirement homes for old royal servants. The large and prosperous houses were bankers to the Crown and creditors to neighbours; the smaller were often their debtors and a prey to neighbours; enmeshed in financial tangles, raising cash by offering risky annuities. They were clearly much less withdrawn from the world than St Benedict and many a later monk-saint would have approved.

Prayers for past, present and future generations and burial in abbey or priory were, for founders and patrons, significant benefits of a spiritual kind for the hereafter. How soon it dawned upon the same founders and patrons that there were benefits to be had of a temporal kind and for the present is difficult to say.

The Cluniac monks of Montacute were obviously prone to outside pressure for, strictly speaking, they were foreigners, usually called aliens, answerable to the abbot of Cluny in far away Burgundy. The monks themselves by the beginning of the fourteenth century were almost certainly all English, but their foreign status made them vulnerable, and particularly so when England and France were at war. The situation was made worse by the ambitious development plans of one or two priors. So on the outbreak of war a group of Edward I's agents took over the monastery on 22 August 1304 and drew up a valuation of assets and liabilities of the prior and his community of 26 monks.

The results were alarming. A total of £34 17s 8d was being spent on what were called liveries, that is daily allowances in food and drink for 12 laymen, and a further £20 was paid out in pensions to 16 laymen. Richard de Salinis, who had both a food allowance and a pension of £4, was probably a retired royal servant and the monks found themselves supporting him 'at the request of the king'. Three other pensions were also paid at royal request. One food allowance, to Edmund the Frenchman, was given at the command of the abbot of Cluny. Some of the liverymen were obviously current servants of the community and were thus being paid wages in kind, but most of the liverymen and 12 of the pensioners, both clerical and lay, came into different categories: five liverymen had paid undisclosed sums to the priory to be fed for life; 12 pensioners were paid 'for laudable services done and to be done for the priory'. Such payments might be sensible for a community in need of political friends, but the sum was nearly half the outgoings of the whole priory; and the king's officers declared that the community was burdened with debts and arrears 'to a total both large and great, the extent of which they did not then know'. Further, the priory church, the refectory, the cloister, houses and other buildings were much ruined and getting worse and could not be repaired for less than £100.

Athelney seems to have been particularly unfortunate with the king's former retainers. In 1304 Gilbert de Ragun presented himself at the monastery with a letter from Edward I ordering the monks to receive him as a pensioner. The monks rather took exception, since already they were providing two other elderly servants with free board and lodging. Another man turned up in 1325 with a similar request from Edward II and two years later a third, appointed to succeed yet another; that is, six men to support, at least two at a time, in less than 30 years. Three other men are known to have been pensioners in the 1340s, successive kings basing their claim on a right to appoint such a man whenever a new abbot was elected and again whenever one of their appointees died. In 1536 the abbey was supporting just one man in this way, named Catecote, who cost 50s a year.

The much richer Glastonbury faced slightly different problems. Perhaps it had been over-generous in its offers of pensions to clergymen, ostensibly in search of livings and needing some help to tide them over. Men from the diocese but also from Salisbury and Lincoln had approached the abbey in that way but in 1241 the abbey realised that several of them were unwilling to give up their pensions even though they had found employment.

It is clear that most of the large monasteries, and some of the smaller ones, too, were burdened by corrodians, men appointed life pensioners usually by the king but occasionally by the head of the house. Nearly a hundred corrodians are known from Glastonbury between the years 1281 and 1537, the most famous of whom was Thomas More, appointed in 1519 and hardly in need of financial support. Many were soldiers. In effect monasteries were being required to pay pensions to government servants. The world was not only at the monastery gates; it was in the monastic treasury as well.

But there were men and women in many monasteries, lay servants either still in employment or retired, for whom a room or two had been set aside as a suitable reward for service. Edmund Gregory at Barlinch in 1536 was probably one of them, Margaret Jobson and John Michel at Cleeve two more. Margaret was a widow and evidently the monastery's cook, for she was repaid in one account for spices and 'other things bought for the use of the household there'. She received bread, ale, candles and fuel, and rent for a house outside the precinct wall. John had a formal contract to dine at the abbot's table or to have a daily allowance of bread, ale, a meat or fish dish, fuel and a room in the monastery.

A third layman at Cleeve was a different sort of resident, a gentleman named Edward Walker. He had agreed with the monastery in 1535 that in return for payment of a capital sum of £27 he would be provided with 'sufficient and holsome' meat and drink at the abbot's table and bread, ale or beer whenever he required it, suitable food for a servant, two rooms under the refectory with access to the cloister, wood for fuel and food and stabling for two horses. All meals might be taken in his room should Edward be ill 'or if it shall please the said Edward for his own singular mind and pleasure'. The deal was an annuity. If Edward died before the £27 was spent, then the abbot gained. In the event he outlived the monastery by almost 30 years. His rooms under the abbey refectory are still to be seen.

8 The home of the community

Buildings

The very earliest days of most monasteries are not recorded well. The year of foundation is very often not known and the details of how the first monks or nuns lived before permanent buildings were provided are simply not available. And when the buildings themselves do not survive, their progress and development are difficult to follow.

All that has been written about the early years of Glastonbury still leaves us in some doubt about the details of its buildings. Archaeologists have tried to reconstruct what was put up by St Dunstan and what by his successors, including the bell tower, chapter house, cloister, refectory, dormitory, infirmary, outer gate, stables and a beautiful building called a *castellum* of dressed stone contributed by Abbot Henry of Blois (1126-71). A disastrous fire in 1184 destroyed most of the works of the Norman abbots Herluin, Thurstan and Henry leaving only a chamber and chapel recently erected by Abbot Robert of Winchester and Abbot Henry's bell tower. The rebuilding began immediately with the Lady Chapel, on the site of the earliest church, which was consecrated in 1186. The monks presumably lived in temporary shelter or at least in buildings the abbey chroniclers thought unworthy of record. Evidently they concentrated attention on the abbey church. The choir, the central tower and the east end of the vaulted nave were finished in the time of Abbot Geoffrey Fromund (1303-22), well over a century after the fire, so that the building could at last be dedicated and used. The great choir screen was built under the tower by Abbot Walter of Taunton (1322-3), and in the next ten years or so Abbot Adam of Sodbury (1322-34) finished the nave, linked it to the Lady Chapel with the Galilee, and began the abbot's great hall. Abbot John of Breinton (1334-42) finished the hall and other nearby rooms, having already, when prior, built a hall and kitchen. Abbot Walter Monington (1342-75) extended the choir eastwards, built a chapel for himself and an infirmary.

That was not the end of building. Abbot John Chinnock (1375-1420) probably rebuilt the cloisters and worked on the dormitory and refectory, for the last of which William Bonville (d.1408) gave £40. Abbot Nicholas Frome (1420-56) built at least part of the great precinct wall. Abbot Richard Bere (1494-1525) created St Joseph's Chapel under the Lady Chapel; had to undertake emergency work in the form of flying buttresses and strainer arches when the central tower threatened to fall; and began the construction of the Edgar Chapel at the east end of the choir, which was magnificently finished by his successor, Abbot Richard Whiting (1525-39). Thus, there were probably few years between the fire in 1184 and the dissolution of the house in 1539 when workmen were not to be heard. And the bewildering list of rooms in the abbey, besides the abbey church, included the abbot's great chamber measuring 72ft long and 24ft broad, the high chamber called the

30 Glastonbury abbey: excavation of the early churches

31 Glastonbury abbey: choir and nave looking west

King's Lodgings, the Bishop's Chamber, the Great Hall on the south side of the cloisters 111ft long and 51ft broad, the convent's kitchen 40ft square, a second kitchen, and 38 other chambers besides halls, chapels, kitchens, parlours and galleries. The surviving ruins at Glastonbury represent just a fraction of what once stood there.

The new cathedral priory at Bath had to be fitted into an existing site in the city when John of Tours transferred his seat there in 1088. The city wall seems to have been moved further east to allow room for the traditional layout of church, cloister and other buildings and also to site the monastic infirmary west of the cloister, conveniently near the hot springs. The monastic precinct thus took in most but not all the south-east quarter of the city and included three churches and a palace for the bishop. About 1279 one of those churches was rebuilt on a different site and the old building converted to a chapel for the bishop.

The church at the heart of the monastery, strictly a cathedral priory because the bishop (and titular abbot) had his Episcopal seat there, was begun by the first bishop of Bath, John of Tours, and at his death in 1122 the vaulting, probably of the choir aisles, was complete. The choir and presbytery were almost certainly roofed by 1135 when Bishop Godfrey was buried on the north side of the high altar. A fire in 1137 evidently did a good deal of damage, but by 1161 and perhaps by 1156 the church was complete, with central and two small western towers, a long nave, short transepts and an apsidal east end with 'bubble' chapels.

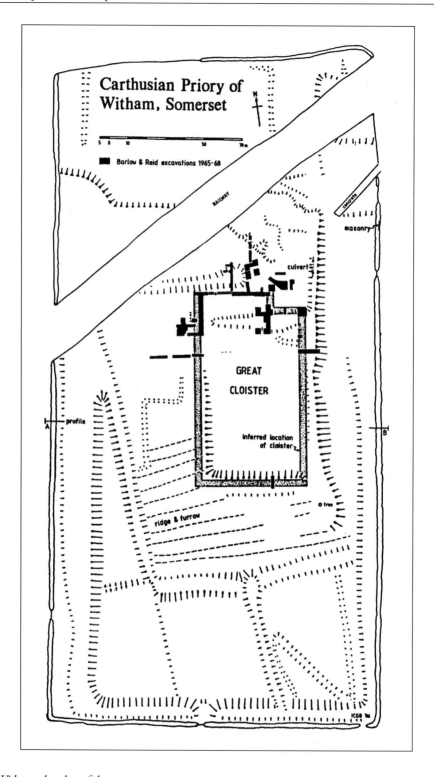

32 Witham, the plan of the monastery

Meanwhile John of Tours had planned a large cloister for a community which never matched his hopes and the fire must have consumed what he built. Under Bishop Robert of Lewes (1136-66), cloister, refectory, dormitory and the rest were rebuilt, in timber on stone footings, and a century later in more permanent stone.

The century which saw building works at Glastonbury and Bath also witnessed the beginnings at Witham, Montacute, Cleeve and Taunton. At Witham the locals were suspicious of the foreigners, the foreigners did not care for local food nor understood local customs. Wooden huts were all the monks had to live in, the weather of Selwood quite unlike that of the French Alps. Then permanent buildings began to rise thanks to money made available by the king's exchequer. Between 1179 and 1187 a total of over £369 was spent specifically on building, in the last year on the monastic church when the cells around the cloister were complete. Not long after the cloister was finished the little stone-vaulted church was erected a mile or so away in the valley where the lay-brothers lived, a building much more reminiscent of Hugh's native Burgundy than Somerset.

Probably the early stages of Montacute and Cleeve were a little different. The founders are likely to have been more directly involved, and the new communities chosen, Montacute's directly from Cluny or perhaps her daughter houses at Lewes or Bermondsey, the other from the Cistercian house at Revesby, some miles south-east of Lincoln. They were less likely to have been sent to barren sites, although they would certainly not have been presented with completed buildings. The most likely scenario is of temporary housing while a beginning was made on the church. The task ahead of each community must have been daunting: with what seems to have been the active support of their founder and his men, the monks of Cleeve, probably established on their site in the Flowery Valley by 1198, were still building their church in 1232 when the king granted them some oak trees to make choir stalls. The east and south ranges of the cloister followed in the second half of the thirteenth century, that is the chapter house, dormitory with day room below, and other rooms including the first refectory with its fine surviving pavement of heraldic tiles. The first buildings of Montacute may not have been of such good quality: in 1276 the buildings were said to have been in bad condition 'and, in fact, almost in ruin', and in 1304 the priory church, the refectory, the cloister and other buildings were 'much in ruin' and could not be repaired for £100.

Progress at Taunton seems to have been almost painfully slow. The same Henry of Blois who was abbot of Glastonbury was also bishop of Winchester and lord of Taunton, and as such granted a new site for the priory outside the town walls. Domestic buildings may have come first, for not until 1277 was it said that the canons had 'begun to build their church in a style of costly magnificence, to the completion of which their means are far from adequate'. But the church was apparently still unfinished in 1337.

Surviving monastic remains in many parts of the county, supplemented by written records, show a continuing enthusiasm for building at monasteries of every size almost until the Dissolution. Abbots were remembered as much for their buildings as for their spiritual leadership. The story of the latest work a Glastonbury has already been told. At Bath Bishop Thomas Bekynton (1443-65) built a new dormitory and Prior John Dunster (1468-81) a new refectory before the inspiration of Bishop Oliver King, which was nothing less than the replacement of the Norman nave of the old cathedral with a

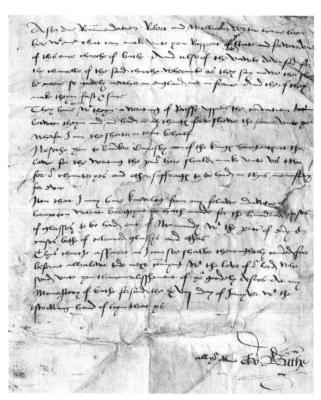

33 Bishop Oliver King describes the building work at Bath, 1503

completely new, but obviously smaller, nave, transepts and choir. The work, under the direction of Henry VII's masons, the brothers Robert and William Vertue, probably began in 1502. The bishop died in the following year, but the new vaulted choir including the delicate chapel in memory of Prior Birde (d.1525) were ready when Bath's last prior, William Holloway, took office after Birde's death. Birde and Holloway between them are given credit for completion of the church, which then probably included a Lady Chapel beyond the choir. One other, equally magnificent addition was the prior's lodging forming the west range of the cloister. Fine oriel windows and decorated chimneys suggest comfortable apartments enjoyed by priors John Cantlow (d.1499) and William Birde (1499-1525).

Surviving buildings elsewhere in the county are evidence of widespread enthusiasm for building in the fifteenth and the earlier sixteenth century, even at small and ill-endowed houses. The fine crossing tower, nave and refectory preserved at Woodspring, for instance, is Perpendicular work of quality, and the fan vaulting in the north chapel at Stavordale is exquisite. The Stavordale work was carried on throughout the fifteenth century, beginning with work on the dormitory substantially paid for by Canon Richard Bruton in 1417, and continuing with the benefaction of John Stourton in 1438, his will declaring that 'the church of Stavordale and the cloister there shall be completed in all things, as well in glazing the windows as in other buildings there to be done, and that the expenses and costs thereof shall be borne by my executors'. And, further, that the whole priory church should be floored with tiles bearing his own and his mother's coats of arms.

34 Part of the unfinished late medieval cloister at Muchelney abbey

The work was finished by 1443 when the suffragan bishop was commissioned to dedicate the nave and chancel of the church. The fine vault over the Jesus chapel on the north side of the church was added by John Zouche, Lord Zouche and St Maur in 1525. Both benefactors wished for burial there and Zouche had, awaiting his end, also built himself a lodging within the priory.

The parlour at Muchelney, with its elaborately carved fireplace and linenfold oak settle, the finest of the chambers on the south-west side of the cloister, seems, by the fragments of glass in its windows, to belong to the time of Abbot Thomas Broke (1505-22); and the embattled gatehouse at Montacute bears the initials of Thomas Chard, prior 1514-32. Abbot David Juyner of Cleeve (1435-66+) seems to have been responsible for the great frater there and Abbot William Dovell (1507-36) with the west range of the cloister, partly paid for by the bequest of £60 from Hugh Roper, vicar of Stogumber.

The buildings of Bruton were converted to a mansion by the Berkeley family soon after its dissolution, and its demolition at the end of the eighteenth century destroyed any possible trace of the buildings Abbot William Gilbert (1496-1533) rebuilt, including a refectory and the Doctor's Chamber mentioned in 1539. Nothing survives, either, of the guest dormitory at Witham, evidence of the increasing popularity of the place for pilgrimage but no charge on the monks themselves because it was the gift of Bishop Thomas Bekynton.

The cost of five centuries and more of building work must have been enormous, and it is clear that maintenance was a burden few houses could easily afford and new works were a luxury which for some spelled financial ruin. To build his new cathedral at Bath, Bishop John of Tours used the income he derived as lord of the city and acquired estates at Claverton which produced the necessary stone, but he and several of his building successors were also obliged to use some of the income of the monks. Benefactors were, as usual, encouraged with offers of spiritual benefits, and in the early fourteenth century a corrody was offered to John Wulfrich in return for service as plumber and glazier. In the 1480s Prior John Cantlow brought a case against his predecessor John Dunster (who had been promoted to be abbot of St Augustine's, Canterbury) for burdening the house with debts of various kinds in order to rebuild the refectory. In the 1530s Bath had at least two permanent salaried superintendents of works, Edward Leycester and John Molton.

Glastonbury, with more resources at its disposal, offered land as payment to craftsmen. Abbot Henry of Blois, for instance, gave Turstin the goldsmith some land which passed to his brother Andrew. By 1189 the task of mending the church's ornaments was exercised by another tenant, a man called Godfrey. In that same year Alwi and Osbert were employed by the abbey as carpenters and the widow of Andrew, the abbey's marbleworker, was listed as one of its tenants. In the middle of the next century, when the abbey church was still under construction, abbey documents refer to Thomas, Herbert, Nicholas, Walter and Robert the masons, and to Roger of Canterbury the glazier. In the early fifteenth century two masons were among Muchelney abbey's tenants on the manor there.

The canons of Taunton, with more slender purses, had to beg, officially: the bishops of Exeter in 1277, of Winchester in 1327, and of Bath and Wells in 1335 each gave licence for collections to be made, and in 1337 an indulgence was offered to all who contributed.

But for the most part, in the absence of information to the contrary, it must be assumed that building, however magnificent, was a charge on the general funds of each house, raised by the sale of corrodies, borrowed against future rents. Cleeve, for example, mortgaged their sheep flock and let their Cornish manors for 90 years in return for much needed cash, and St John's hospital, Wells, borrowed the large sum of £113, part of it an entry fine for a long lease of Keinton Mandeville manor, specifically for repairs. The surviving accounts for the last years of Somerset's monasteries are not always easy to interpret and the accusations of the king's visitors need to be treated with caution, but it is not difficult to believe, for instance, that given the vast amount of building at Bath in the 1530s, the abbey should have been £400 in debt.

Places of prayer

Twelve of the 73 chapters of the Rule of St Benedict are concerned with the Divine Office, the regular singing of the night and morning services and of offices throughout the day at Prime, Terce, Sext, None, Vespers and Compline, at which the Psalms were sung in regular rotation accompanied with prayers, hymns and readings from Scripture. Regular performance of the Divine Office was an essential part of the life of each community and the choir of each monastic church, its rows of stalls facing each other before the high altar, was at the heart of every religious community. The Rule allowed large communities to sing antiphonally, that is, those on one side of the choir singing a verse of each Psalm followed by those on the other side singing the next. Many monks discovered an aptitude for singing, normally unaccompanied by an organ; while some became scholars or administrators, others found fulfilment in being choir monks whose regular duties were by nature almost anonymous: office holders were mentioned often enough in financial statements but choir monks appear only when the whole community is named.

For some monks, probably never satisfactorily taught as novices, the liturgy became meaningless. 'Muche rendering of the salter cannot intend their lernyng', complained some young monks from Athelney in 1538, 'syngyngmen of the howse be light falows and causeth muche lousines emoyg religious men . . . ther servyce in the churche is very tedius . . . it shuld be more necessary to have a scolemaster to instruct theym than to have soo many singingmen as they have.' 'Divine service is so tedious that the brethren cannot have time to study scripture' was a similar complaint from Glastonbury. Perhaps there really was a wider problem: more emphasis on music and singing in other parts of the monastic church, undertaken by laymen and boys, and thus, in the eyes of the religious, a diminution in the importance of the regular liturgy.

Certainly there was pressure from benefactors, patrons and pilgrims so that in all but the smallest monastic churches, large or small chapels were built and furnished so that masses might be said or sung, or images erected for special devotions. The names of benefactors are not known, but somewhere in the priory church at Montacute six daily masses were celebrated, three sung and three said. An agreement at Athelney drawn up in 1384 between the abbot and Elizabeth Blount involved a permanent endowment for a priest, either a monk or one from outside the community, to say mass every day 'with special collects common and secret' in the abbey church choir at the high altar before the Trinity (except only Good Friday) for Elizabeth herself and 21 members of her family, all Christians to whom Elizabeth was somehow indebted, all her benefactors, and for all Christian souls who were in pain in purgatory.

There were, no doubt, similar foundations at altars in chapels in other houses. The Norman church at Muchelney, for instance, taking the place of the apsidal eighth-century building over which the new choir was built, had an apsidal east end with bubble chapels on its east, north and south sides. There was a similar apsidal chapel to the east of the south transept. A rectangular Lady Chapel, developed for the increasing devotion to the Virgin Mary, took the place of the former east end in the later fourteenth century. Taunton priory church by the end of the fifteenth century had a chapel of St Anthony, an aisle dedicated to St Botulph, a chapel of the Virgin Mary by the cloister, and another of Our Lady and St Theodoric in the churchyard. Somewhere in the building was the Trinity door, presumably one with a representation of the Trinity above it, and somewhere else an image of Our Lady of Pity.

The arrangements Abbot Adam of Sodbury made for himself, his parents and his friend Prior John of Breinton in 1333 envisaged eight chaplains or clerks with good voices and divided into choirs who would serve the Lady Chapel 'devoutly in song and melody' and should be involved with the daily office of the dead. On solemn festivals they were to join the monks in the great choir.

So it was in subsidiary services held outside the monastic choir that organists and singing men were to be found. In 1349 Ralph Drake began work at Muchelney as cantor, his duties to sing high mass and to teach four boys and a monk to play on the organ. William Cupper, described both as singingman and organist, was employed at Bath in the late 1530s, first receiving lodgings and food in the monastery and later, when he was married with a daughter, occupying an abbey property outside. Thomas Foxe was appointed in 1538 as cantor or clerk of the (Lady) chapel to teach song to boys and organ to any monk who wished to learn. He, too, was a layman, and received as wages £5, a house, fuel and a gown.

Glastonbury had a long tradition of music and organs, but complaints from the abbot in the fifteenth century illustrate the tension between choir monks and lay musicians. St Dunstan when Archbishop of Canterbury, on one of his many visits to his old home, had an organ built for the abbey. William le Orgonistre was employed in 1322 as clerk in the Lady Chapel. That chapel, built immediately after the fire of 1184 where the ancient church of wattles had stood for so long, was a particular focus of devotion, at first to the Virgin and from the 1490s to St Joseph of Arimathia. The contract agreed in 1534 with James Reynyger made clear that his first duty was in the Lady Chapel at daily mattins, masses, evensong, compline and 'anteymes'. He was also to 'do service' in singing and playing the organ in the choir of the abbey church on feasts and festivals; to teach six boys in pricksong and descant and two to play the organ; the convent was to find 'clavyngecordes'.

Calling to worship

As well as giving Glastonbury an organ, St Dunstan had had a bell cast for the refectory. A regular regimen needed bells to summon brethren and sisters from cloister or garden to the office in the choir; bells to tell workers in field or byre that the community was again at prayer; bells to welcome festivals and holy days. Glastonbury, of course, had more than others; in 1189 the community seems to have employed two *pulsatores* and 17 *sonatores*, which appears to mean ringers and strikers. In the 1320s there were 12 bells, evidently divided between two towers, described as the church tower and the clock tower. Roger de Worthi made an agreement with the sacrist about them and listed them by name: Mary, Peter, Paul, Edmund, Thomas, Martin and Nicholas in one tower, Gabriel, Dunstan, Benignus, Katherine and Margaret in the other. Eleven of those bells were given by Abbot Adam of Sodbury (1323-34), and the ringers in the bell tower were paid 2s for their efforts on his anniversary. Seven of Sodbury's bells, John Leland was told two centuries later, were then still surviving.

At the Dissolution bells were of interest to the king's officers because they were worth money. They thus appear in the accounts of the king's officials: there was just one at Buckland, four at Worspring, five at Barlinch, seven at Cleeve and four at the chapel of St Mary at Chapel Cleeve. There were seven at Keynsham for which Francis Edwards paid £72 7s 6d. Those were all modest houses so the 12 at Glastonbury might not have been unusual.

Decorative arts

John of Glastonbury's chronicle of his community, written in the early fourteenth century, recorded the gifts of a mighty army of benefactors from the time of King Ine (d.726) onwards who bestowed, besides large tracts of land, a dazzling quantity of precious objects. Ine's donation, to beautify the church he built there to add to the three churches already on the site, dedicated to the Saviour and the apostles Peter and Paul, comprised:

> A silver chapel constructed of 2,640lb of silver, and an altar of 264lb of gold; a chalice and paten of 10lb of gold; a thurible of 8lb and 20 mancusses of gold; candlesticks of $12\frac{1}{2}$ pounds of silver; illumination for the texts of the Gospel of 20lb and 6 mancusses of gold; vessels for water and other altar-vessels of 17lb of gold; basins of 8lb of gold; and the holy-water vessel of 20lb of silver. He also made images of the Lord, of blessed Mary, and of the 12 apostles, of 175lb of silver and 28lb of gold, and the altar cloths and sacerdotal vestments, subtly woven throughout with gold and precious stones.

The precise details sound as suspicious as the charter granted by the same king; and the assumed destruction of monastic treasures in Viking raids could well be used to explain the failure of such early magnificence to survive.

Yet clearly Glastonbury was the recipient of much generosity, the most munificent the legacy of Abbot Henry of Blois which included besides vestments, a golden banner, a great orphrey, a whole plethora of holy relics, a precious tapestry of Saracen workmanship and a crystal lion enclosing the hair of St John the Evangelist.

Abbot Adam of Sodbury (1323-34) gave gold and silver chalices, cups and other liturgical plate; magnificent vestments in red, green, purple, indigo, yellow embroidered with animals, birds, heraldry and religious symbols in gold and silver. Such an amazing collection of precious things needed expert care and in 1260 a man named William Goldsmith held office to mend all goldsmith's work in the church and to repair all bowls, goblets and spigots in the refectory.

Less than three centuries later the abbey was no more and all its riches taken by a grasping king. Thomas Cromwell noted the removal of more than 11,000oz of plate besides gold, rich copes and, among jewels delivered to the king's Master of Jewels, 'a super altar called the Great Sapphire of Glastonbury'. That last, of silver and gold, probably included the jewel which had been brought to Glastonbury by St David and which for long had been hidden in a door of St Mary's church. Abbot Henry of Blois had recognised it and mounted it with gold, silver and precious stones. There were also items of mother-of-pearl and coral.

Glastonbury's tangible riches were far greater than those of any Somerset neighbour but Bath boasted in the late tenth or early eleventh century mass robes and two gilt crosses given by Wulfaru, and the body of St Euphemia, the mitre and amice of St Peter of Tarentaise, and an alb of cloth of gold given in 1180 by Bishop Reginald FitzJocelin.

In the 1480s Prior John Cantlow accused his predecessor John Dunster of making away with two large silver basins, gilded inside, a set of 12 silver platters, dishes and saucers, and three chargers, presumably all from the priory refectory, and perhaps from the prior's own chapel or else from the priory treasury a set of silver and gilt sacred vessels: two cruets, a silver pax, a chalice and a flagon. He was accused of disposing of a pair of mass vestments given to Bath by Bishop Thomas Bekynton and a salt cellar and bason, also of silver, formerly in the refectory.

The Cluniacs, Cistercians and Carthusians performed a much simpler liturgy and their limited means would hardly stretch to extravagance even if they so wished, though gifts of the faithful would probably not have been refused. At the Dissolution Cleeve seems to have possessed only two sets of mass vestments worth selling, one 'de lez purple velvet', the other 'de lez whyte Damaske' and their sacred vessels weighed only 74oz. The sisters of Buckland had even less, their plate weighing 9 oz. But Barlinch had silverware amounting to 203oz, Woodspring 321oz, and Cannington 365oz.

Places of pilgrimage

Glastonbury had relics of great sanctity given by successive kings. Alfred gave a fragment of the True Cross; his son Edward the Elder (899-924) and his grandson Athelstan (924-39) contributed to an incomparable collection which included 'part of the hole where the Lord's Cross stood' and 'some of the stones where Jesus stood when he ascended into heaven'.

Edgar (959-75) 'loved the church of Glastonbury above all others, added to it great possessions, and was watchful in all things which pertained to the church's honour and convenience, both within its walls and outside'. Among his gifts were a gold and silver cross, his coronation robe, a precious shrine with the relics of St Vincent and the head of St Apollinaris, relics of other saints, another fragment of the Cross, part of Christ's tunic, a piece of St Peter's beard, parts of the staffs of Moses and Aaron.

To those ancient religious relics the community at Glastonbury added special attractions. The house had not been mentioned in a list of English pilgrimage places in the eleventh century but by the fourteenth it was firmly established. Its chronicler John of Glastonbury told of how foreigners wanted samples of its earth against the time of their own burials and could not understand why English pilgrims travelled to foreign shrines when they had such a holy place at home. By the late fourteenth century a guidebook for pilgrims had been compiled, telling the stories of Arthur and Joseph of Arimathia. With John of Glastonbury recording the hundreds of days of indulgence available for pilgrims and describing the wonders to be seen at the abbey, the success of the abbey's publicity drive was assured. Early in the sixteenth century a second guide book was produced, this time printed, which described the wonders visitors could see including the Glastonbury Thorn and a remarkable walnut tree.

35 *The fourteenth-century 'Catalogue of Saints Resting in England' includes several buried at Glastonbury*

36 St Joseph of Arimathia in the east window of Langport church

The account book of William Cholmeley, cofferer of Edward Stafford, duke of Buckingham, suggests that the duke joined the band of pilgrims to Glastonbury, staying at the abbey as befitted his station, for several days at the end of April 1521. He offered 6s 8d to the shrine of Joseph of Arimathia on the 29th, gave the same sum at high mass and 3s 4d 'to the holy relics there' on the next day, and another 3s 4d to Joseph's shrine on 1 May. There were also payments 'to an idiot of the abbey', to one of the abbot's servants whose bow was broken by one of the duke's men, and small gifts to two of the abbot's household who had evidently provided entertainment, a French poet and a harper. Some three weeks later Cholmeley paid 3s 4d to an 'arasman' of the abbot, presumably a weaver of decorative hangings whose work he had admired in the abbot's lodgings.

Visits of lesser folk are not recorded in such detail, and critical Royal Injunctions issued in 1538 noted that pilgrims coming to visit the increasingly popular shrine of St Joseph were not being given anything in the way of religious instruction. The cures recorded in the poem called 'The Lyfe of Joseph of Armathia' might be seen either as astute advertising or attempts at serious teaching; it is difficult to be certain.

Bath, curiously, was never so popular in the Middle Ages as it had been in Roman times. Archbishop Theobald of Canterbury (1139-61) offered 20 days indulgence to all who visited the great cross there on the feast of the Exaltation and Bishop Reginald (d.1191) gave the community the body of St Euphemia and vestments belonging to St Peter of Tarantaise, but they do not seem to have become significant objects of veneration. The altar and image of the Trinity in the abbey church attracted a following in the fifteenth century if not earlier, a following popular enough to be condemned in 1459 by a local Lollard.

No other monastery in Somerset could hope to compete with Glastonbury's attractions, but Cleeve possessed the chapel of St Mary by the Sea which had been part of its original foundation in 1198. It was situated to the north of the monastery on the Bristol Channel coast under a cliff near a place now called Blue Anchor. About 1398 it was seriously damaged, presumably by storm, and both the pope and the bishop of Exeter offered indulgences to all who would contribute to its repair. More serious damage was done in 1452 when the cliff collapsed and only the statue of the Virgin survived intact. It was rebuilt in 1455 by Abbot Juyner on a safer site further inland, at a place now called Chapel Cleeve, and then or later a 'hostel' to shelter pilgrims was built nearby. Part of the building still survives in the mansion known as Chapel Cleeve. The new dormitory built at Witham at about the same time at the expense of Bishop Bekynton was almost certainly to provide quarters for pilgrims visiting the increasingly popular monks there.

The duke of Buckingham, travelling from Thornbury to Glastonbury in 1521 first made offerings at Keynsham, and may have called at the charterhouse at Hinton as well as Keynsham again on his way home. James Hadley of Withycombe, a local gentleman, regretting that he had never been on pilgrimage, in 1532 left small sums of money to the famous shrines of England — Canterbury, Hailes, Windsor, Shorne and Walsingham — but he left a much larger sum to the shrine of the Blessed Lady of Cleeve. John Leland, visiting ten years later, described Abbot Juyner's chapel as 'well builded' and the hostel as 'goodly', but by then there were no more pilgrims.

Yet popular pilgrimage brought difficult pressures. Abbot Nicholas Frome of Glastonbury in 1455 petitioned the pope to allow him to present for ordination younger men than normal and more than the usual number each year because there were not enough priests in the community — he blamed 'mortalities and other misfortunes' — to say the divine office required by the 'great multitude' of people who came to visit. Probably that same abbot realised that pilgrims needed beds to sleep in as well as collecting boxes for their alms. To that end he built an inn not far from the main entrance to the abbey, called the George, and enjoyed a reasonable rent from the property. Two or three doors away was the Crown inn, one of the few buildings in the centre of the town owned by outsiders — the canons of Bruton. Pilgrimage was potentially good business, but actually how successful? Not every visitor to Glastonbury was so generous as the duke of Buckingham. The abbey receiver for the year 1503-4 recorded only £4 5s 9d given in alms; in 1535 the takings in St Joseph's box were reckoned at £6 13s 4d a year.

9 The comforts of home

St Benedict foresaw that monks would live by his Rule in climates both colder and warmer than his own and the abbot of each community was instructed to take the local climate into consideration. What were essential were a tunic, a cowl (thin or thick according to season), a scapular for work, stockings and shoes. In course of time those who followed his Rule came to wear black clothing and came to be known as Black Monks to distinguish them from their brethren of the Cistercian family whose clothing, as St Benedict had originally decreed, was locally produced, often coarse and undyed — hence their name White Monks. The Carthusians, the Augustinian canons and the Dominican friars also wore black, the Franciscan friars brown.

The dormitory

Accommodation, according to the Rule, came before food and clothing. If possible, St Benedict had directed, monks should sleep each in his own bed and if not in a single dormitory then by tens or twenties, with seniors in charge in rooms lit all night by a single candle. Bedding, adequate for the place and the season, was to be mattress, blanket, coverlet and pillow. The austere dormitory at Cleeve reveals, on close inspection, what was to become the norm; that for reasons of comfort and privacy some kind of cubicle had been built around each bed. It is unlikely that either the inclination or the funds at Cleeve ever stretched to the luxury which Bishop Ralph of Shrewsbury found at Muchelney in 1335 where the simple bed-surrounds had been transformed into separate and often ornate chambers.

So the simple common life was inevitably transformed and personal privilege and private property were permitted, whatever the bishop might say. Thus in 1401 Robert Wynchestre, a member of the community at Athelney, obtained permission from the Pope to retain for life the room he had previously been assigned by his abbot, probably as an office from which to carry out some duty in the house. Further, without asking permission of his abbot, he was empowered to dispose of any private property he may have acquired during the course of his work and any money he might have accumulated.

Robert Wynchestre, though never abbot, was obviously a man of influence. Richard Springe resigned his office as prior at Woodspring in 1525 when he was over 90 years of age. In the mood of the times his retirement package was still generous: he was given two servants, a room in Locking, his own room in the priory with another room next to it, his own privy, a barn and a garden. There was, since the number of canons had dwindled, plenty of room available.

37 The thirteenth-century dormitory range at Cleeve abbey on the east side of the cloister and the new refectory on the south above rooms for corrodians

The refectory

St Benedict's feeling about food was flexible provided that over-indulgence and indigestion were avoided; the Rule, after all, came to be adapted for many different countries and climates. One or two meals at the sixth or the ninth hour with two cooked dishes for choice and fresh fruit or vegetables in addition were his suggestion, with a pound weight of bread each a day. The sick might eat red meat to strengthen them; the fit should not.

The practice at Glastonbury in the earlier twelfth century as described by William of Malmesbury shows how far changes had been made. On some days of the week three main dishes of eggs or fish were served at each table and two small dishes called pittances were added to be shared between one or two monks; on others there were two main dishes and three pittances. On holy days there were more dishes, mead, wine and wheat cakes; on special festivals even more dishes. And why not? Abbot Henry of Blois left money at his death in 1171 to provide salmon, honey and wine on special occasions because, as a later monk explained, 'a suitable bestowal of bodily necessities usually encourages monks in the divine service and to a very great extent eliminates the hateful cause of grumbling'.

Grumbling might well arise over food. Bishop Droxford heard about troubles at Bath in 1321 where the prior's financial extravagance had reduced spending in the kitchen. At Keynsham in the 1350s it was not so much a question of quality and quantity but of meals no longer being taken together, of irregular accounting by the cook, and of lay people interrupting meals which had once been an opportunity for the whole community to hear the reading in silence.

38 Glastonbury, the abbot's kitchen

A century later Bishop Bekynton's visitations at Taunton and Bruton drew attention to the poor quality of bread, beer and cheese; and the elderly and sick prior of Athelney was allowed to eat meat even on days he said Mass, because the number of monks at the house was so small that he found himself saying divine office most weeks of the year. In 1525 the retiring prior of Woodspring was given as his pension a double portion of the allowance of meat and fish at dinner and supper, and each week 14 white loaves, 12 gallons of ale, and a cheese supplied from Locking village.

As for clothing, there was simply the question of weather. Who but the most saintly could pray and meditate when the weather was cold, the cell draughty and clothing inadequate? Tunic, cowl, scapular for work, stockings and shoes were recommended, but since the monk slept in his day clothes, then two of each to allow for one being washed was proper.

Young Popham, a novice at Glastonbury in 1309, was fitted out with $9\frac{1}{2}$ ells of black russet cloth for his robes and a sleeveless tunic, black serge stockings, fur linings for his supertunica and his hood, shoes and a maniple, the whole costing 22s 9d. He was perhaps too young to require a night cap and a shaving cloth which were among the 31 items every Ely monk found necessary in the early sixteenth century. At about the same time Andrew, a member of the rather more strict and simple Carthusians, came from London to Witham with a habit comprising a 'kyrtyll' and a cowl, a 'stamen' cowl and shirt, a pair of 'nete' stockings and a pair of socks and, as some deference to the Selwood winter, a woollen cowl, two caps and a lined coat. For more comfort he brought a pillow and a shaving cloth. Summer in the far west was likely to be warmer, and part of the benefaction of Gilbert of

39 The Rule of St Benedict, chapter 55, 'On the Clothes and shoes of the brethren'

Woolavington was 60s payable to the monk porter of Cleeve to pay for 'summer' cloth to make 15 cowls.

Poverty might well put a limit on adequate clothing and in 1234 the king gave orders that each of the sisters at Buckland should have a tunic and a pair of slippers. Brother Peter, one of the chaplains belonging to the preceptory there, was given the sum of 20s in 1317 'to mend his habit from year to year while it lasts'.

All the monks at Glastonbury presumably benefited from the papal privilege granted in 1248 of having skull caps, a grant made after Abbot Michael of Amesbury had told the Holy Father how particularly cold the abbey was, the prey of biting winds blowing without let or hindrance across icy levels.

And when those winds seemed to blow colder and became more penetrating, who would begrudge Thomas Byrde, retiring prior of Barlinch in 1524, in recognition of his service, a pension of £6 13s 4d, 20 white loaves a week, 12 gallons of ale, two canonical portions of food, a linen rochet, a habit every fourth year, sufficient wood for his room and 1lb of candles every week and to occupy the second best chamber in the house? And who would not agree that, since both young and old suffered from cold in the church of St John's hospital at Bridgwater, that the early morning mass in wintertime should begin at 6 o'clock instead of 5 o'clock ?

10 The value of divine study

St Benedict saw each monastery as 'a school for the service of the Lord' where each monk living under the Rule would persevere in the religious life according to God's teaching and his own strength of purpose. Newcomers to the life, novices, during the period before taking formal vows, were assigned special quarters to study, eat and sleep under the care of a senior monk. Boys and girls coming first to the monastic life would thus have to be taught reading and singing before they could take a full part in the daily and nightly offices or read to the community during meals and at other times of the day. Studying books in the monastic library or going to university might follow. Probably every Somerset house therefore had some means of training novices at least to the standard needed for choir monks and nuns.

Schools

So much has to be inferred, that the rare record of John, a boy at Glastonbury school in the 1320s, is a triumph. He was evidently so influenced by his tutor John of Worcester that he moved to his tutor's former home by the Severn and took his name.

Glastonbury's school recorded in 1377 was certainly not for novices. In that year a tax was paid for 39 'clerks' there. Only one of them, John Staple, certainly became a monk and was still in the house in 1413. Five, John Leycester, William Modeford, John Hore, Robert FitzJames and John Vrye or Frye became parish priests in the diocese; two others, Nicholas Barwe and John Thomas, seem to have lived at Wedmore and may never have proceeded beyond minor orders; one more, William Sandel, may have found employment in the consistory court at Wells.

Perhaps a little later in the fifteenth century Jenkin Henbury, heir to a small property in Bovetown, was sent to the almonry school at Glastonbury. He did not follow a clerical or monastic career but was apprenticed to a prominent citizen of Wells. One other Glastonbury schoolboy is known. He was Richard Bere, a nephew of the abbot, who went on to study at Oxford about 1493 and later became a member of the London Charterhouse. There in May 1537 he refused to take the oath acknowledging the king's supremacy and was imprisoned at Newgate where he died of starvation nearly three months later.

Just before the Dissolution, reports from Glastonbury's school were not happy. There were complaints in 1538 that novices had to pay 20s quarterly for their schoolmaster, that the convent lacked books of scripture and time to study the same, and that the schoolmaster received poor pay. Between Easter and Whitsun, it was said, there was not public reading of any scripture in the house and for lack of lectures, brethren played at dice and cards. The prior and cook were actually said to have been against learning.

There were school masters or grammar masters at Bath and Cleeve in the years before the Dissolution, and complaints from Keynsham in 1526 and Athelney in 1538 that there were none. The four novices at Keynsham in 1526 asked that they might have instruction in grammar and one of the senior canons regretted that no one at the time was at university, although it had long been the tradition of the house, so he claimed, to send scholars there. Athelney monks in 1538 declared that they 'wold raither that they shuld [have a] scolemaster to teach them ther grammar to lern scripture' and the abbot was ordered to allow the brethren to have two hours every weekday for reading and study.

The very small and poor Barlinch put other houses to shame where at some date probably soon after 1500 but possibly as early as 1480 Master David Juyne was teaching Latin to a pupil who may well have been William Nicholas. Fragments of William's school book, later used in the bindings of records of the Luttrell family, reveal Master David's teaching methods and William's progress using English proverbs, riddles and jokes to be translated into Latin. William, who may have been a novice or equally well an outside pupil, began his studies early from Monday and Friday, but seems to have been brought in one Saturday perhaps to complete an imposition. Master David was not a canon of the house but evidently used the premises with the canons' approval. He was not there by 1509 for injunctions issued after visitation required that the house find someone to teach grammar to the canons.

By 1298 until 1535 or later the hospital of St John in Bridgwater had no school on the premises but operated rather like a hall at a medieval university. It was home to 13 poor scholars on the foundation of Robert Burnell, former bishop of Bath and Wells. Those scholars attended the town school and, at the time of the foundation, the hospital also provided food for another seven pupils.

Universities

Over the period from the later thirteenth century to the Dissolution, Oxford college and university records show a steady stream of men, most of them Benedictines, Franciscans and Dominicans, studying at the college belonging to their order, presumably after initial training in their own communities.

The numbers from Somerset are small and even the relatively large number from Glastonbury represents little more on average than one man in every generation. Until 1500, 25 Glastonbury monks are known to have been at Oxford, some of them certainly at Gloucester (later Worcester) college, the college established by the Benedictines for members of their Order. Five each went from Bath and Muchelney, some if not all to Canterbury college; Taunton, Keynsham and Bruton each sent three, presumably to the Augustinians' St Mary's college, founded in the 1440s. The sole known scholar from Montacute is unnamed but cost the priory 26s 8d in 1538-9.

Between 1500 and the Dissolution greater numbers suggest that the heads of some Somerset monasteries, still led by Glastonbury, took learning much more seriously:

40 Glastonbury students' rooms at Gloucester (now Worcester) college, Oxford

41 Sinesius Cyrenensis, fifteenth-century copy given to the monk Peter Weston by Abbot John Selwood

Glastonbury sent at least ten men to Oxford in those last 40 years, four in the single year 1529-30, two of those and two more in the year 1532-3; Bruton sent four after 1500, Bath, Cleeve, Montacute, Taunton and the Bridgwater Franciscans one each. Seven out of those 18 graduated as bachelors in theology.

Heads of houses reported their graduates to visitors as a matter of pride, though the process often gave rise to jealousy on the part of those left behind. Bruton in 1539 boasted two bachelors in divinity, a bachelor in law, and a scholar still at Oxford. At the same time there was a bachelor in divinity at Bath, and a scholar from Montacute was also supported at Oxford.

But if abbots and priors boasted, fellow monks and canons were less happy. Several of his fellows left behind at Glastonbury complained that John Neot had been at Oxford as the perpetual student for 12 years 'and litle doth perfect in his lernyng'.

Libraries

> And in these days of Lent they shall each receive a book from the library, which they shall read straight through from the beginning.

The Rule of St Benedict did not regard reading as a penance, of course; but rather saw Lent as a special opportunity to study. Reading was ordered in summer between the fourth and the sixth hours and after a meal a monk might choose either to rest on his bed or to read quietly without disturbing others. In winter reading was to be done up to the end of the second hour when Terce was to be sung and again after None except in Lent, when monks should be so occupied from morning until the end of the third hour. And woe betide a brother 'who spends his time in idleness or gossip and does not apply himself to the reading'; one or two of the seniors were ordered to be on patrol.

There still survive in libraries, mostly in Oxford, Cambridge and London, but also as far away as Dublin, Paris, New York and Princeton, nearly a hundred books which once

42 *Page from St Augustine's* Exposition of the Apocalypse *of the tenth century formerly in Glastonbury abbey library, the copy ordered to be made by St Dunstan*

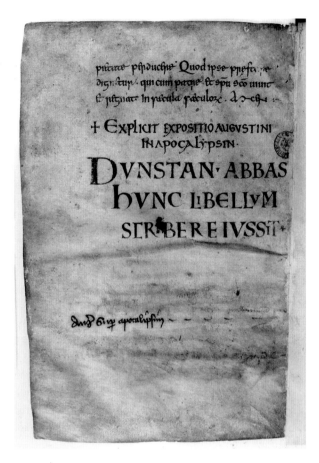

belonged to Somerset religious communities. Those represent a fraction of the books which for centuries had been the main sources of learning, the total of which will never be known. Glastonbury's library was evidently the largest in the county, having nearly 500 volumes in 1247-8 covering history, theology, science, philosophy, medicine, lives of saints and service books. And Witham's must have been substantial after about 1459 when John Blacman brought with him well over 60 books.

John Leland, an expert in such matters and acting in some sort of official capacity for Henry VIII, left records of his many visits to monastic libraries in search of important books. He first went to Glastonbury some time in the late 1530s where he knew he would find the best collection of ancient texts. Even so he was rather overcome by what he found:

> Scarcely had I crossed the threshold when the mere sight of the most ancient books took my mind with an awe or stupor of some kind, and for that reason I stopped in my tracks a little while. Then having paid my respects to the deity of the place, I examined all the bookcases for some days with the greatest interest.

The result of his study was a list of 44 titles, at least 30 of which could have dated from before 1100, including works by Bede and St Aldhelm and volumes concerning King Arthur, Merlin and St Dunstan. Of those 30 some had been at Glastonbury before the Norman Conquest and are among those still surviving, including one actually made at Glastonbury and now at the Bodleian library in Oxford. It is a work by St Augustine which bears the inscription 'Abbot Dunstan ordered this book to be written' and includes a drawing of the abbot prostrate at the feet of Christ.

Another survival from Glastonbury, but only a fragment because the book was broken up and a few pages were used to repair and strengthen an estate survey, had once been a book which might well have been in the monastic library when Dunstan himself was studying there: a work by Isidore of Seville which probably originated in Ireland or was copied by an Irish scholar.

How many of Glastonbury's books were actually produced or copied in the library is unknown but Elyas *luminator* was employed there *c*.1260. Nicholas Faux, who probably entered the house in the early 1370s and was still there in 1404 was a transcriber of theological works.

The library at Bath, not as large as that at Glastonbury, was still an important one. It had suffered at an early stage when Abbot Saewold removed 33 volumes to Normandy soon after the Conquest, but Bishop John of Tours, a medical scholar of repute, left most of his books to the monastery. Leland, who recorded only six books in his survey, mentioned others including works by Bath's greatest student-scholar, Adelard, and the fact that several Bath books were given by King Athelstan. Bath's library was evidently strong in medicine and science. And one book seen by Leland, a text dating back to the ninth century, was so attractive that it was removed to the king's library in 1533, six years before the Dissolution. Two years later Prior William Holloway sent another gem, the works of St Anselm, to Thomas Cromwell as some kind of bribe.

There still survive one volume from Athelney, 14 from Bath, two from the Franciscan convent of Bridgwater, one from Bruton and so on, probably no reflection of the size of each collection. The six survivals from Hinton and the 16 from Witham suggest, however, that the Carthusians took their studies seriously, and Witham's 16 included some of the 24 titles formerly belonging to John Blacman. The Carthusians of Hinton lent several of their books to another house of the Order in 1343 and in the early sixteenth century borrowed nine from the London Charterhouse, most of them contemplative works, some of German origin.

Not all the books in monastic libraries were works of theology, history, philosophy, law, science or medicine. There were bibles, as might be expected, psalters and other works connected with the services of the church, and improving literature like lives of saints. But Glastonbury and other house owned collections of riddles and Bath's library included a volume which Leland described as a 'book of antiquities' which has been recognised as the cartulary or collection of copies of land charters which found its way to the library of Corpus Christi college, Cambridge.

The original charters recording all kinds of legal business may not have been kept in every monastic library but perhaps separately, by the head of each house along with accounts, surveys, rentals and court rolls, the records of each separate estate. Such records have survived in very great numbers, for they were of use to the buyers of monastic estates at the Dissolution. In theory these records should have passed to the new owners, but many evidently did not reach the government department which was trying to collect them and many others did not leave that department when new owners were found. The result, for instance, is that the Public Record Office in Kew still has the accounts drawn up for the last whole year of Glastonbury's life which enabled the king's accountants to arrive at a price for each property.

In practice prospective purchasers short-circuited the system. Sir John Thynne of Longleat, bidder for the former Glastonbury estate of Walton, 'had oute' of the abbey 'bookes, munimentes, transcriptes and writinges' before they could be transferred to London. Many are still preserved by his successors at Longleat including the largest collection of Glastonbury account and court rolls and several cartularies. The Lord Treasurer requested in 1555 that he should hand them over and was ignored.

The story that another buyer of a Glastonbury manor, John Horner, behaved similarly seems unlikely. There is still at least one abbey account roll at Mells Manor, dating from the year 1515-16 when Richard Whiting, the future abbot, was receiver of the monastery, but there are no Mells accounts and Horner, a long-time tenant of the manor, would have little need of records to assess the value of his purchase or establish his right to it. His deal with the Crown in 1543, for the large cash sum of £1,831 19s 11¼d, seems to have been entirely above board, so what gave rise to the nursery rhyme is a mystery.

Theology, law, philosophy and history might seem to have been the most appropriate subjects for study by religious, but astronomy and arithmetic came within the embrace of any who pursued a degree at university. Adelard of Bath, the first English scientist, received little of the learning he later acquired from the city that gave him his name, though he was almost certainly a Somerset man by birth and may well have begun his career in the Benedictine house there. Almost from the other end of the Middle Ages, the county may have given birth to the astronomer and chronicler John Somer, a member of the Franciscan community at Bridgwater. Somer was patronised by the rich and famous, mentioned by Chaucer, employed by the royal family, and only concentrated on theology towards the end of his life. Thomas Cory, a monk at Muchelney by 1431 and subprior by 1463, also made astronomical tables based on the work of Somer and others, and writers in the sixteenth century still remembered Somer's horoscopes and star catalogues.

Another memory was perhaps even more significant. John Leland recorded among his notes about Glastonbury that Abbot Richard Bere gave to his community *lectura antiqui operis*. Bere himself had been as a diplomat to Italy and is known to have been a correspondent of the scholar Erasmus of Rotterdam, who recognised in him a man sympathetic to the New Learning of the Renaissance. It seems, in this Latin phrase, that Bere intended that his fellow monks should be encouraged to realise the significance of the Classical treasures in their library.

11 In support of holiness

St Benedict had recognised that there was a difference between the needs of small communities and of large ones. There were clearly practical tasks which needed to be done, and not all monks were evidently skilled in that way. An abbot, he declared, would need to appoint a cellarer to have charge of 'everything', that is of the food and drink to feed both the community and the sick, children, guests and the poor. And in a large house the cellarer might need help to carry out his duties and would be excused having to serve in the kitchen. St Benedict also saw the need for one or more monks to be responsible for tools, clothing and other articles the monastery owned, another to serve for a year at a time in charge of the kitchen for the abbot and his guests, and another to be in charge of the guest house and the gatehouse.

Times and circumstances changed. To feed and clothe the large community at Glastonbury, to carry out religious duties, to maintain buildings, and to administer its huge estate efficiently required organisational skills, legal and farming expertise, and financial acumen of a high order, let alone a pool of labour which itself needed skill and proper payment. While still clearly in charge, the abbot of Glastonbury had to devolve many of his duties to what became almost independent departments inside the abbey, most of them with income of their own separate from that of the abbey itself. The head of each department was, of course, a man under obedience (the generic name was obedientiaries), but within the terms of his office he acted independently.

As early as 1189, under the abbacy of Henry de Sully, there were 12 monastic managers, each charged with separate duties involving the liturgy, the welfare of members of the community, the food supply and responsibilities towards the needy. Archbishop John Pecham of Canterbury, a Franciscan and a reformer, found when he visited Glastonbury in 1281 that the abbey was deeply in debt and there was a danger that the abbey's departments would become almost independent organisations. He therefore ordered that some kind of central financial control should be arranged under a treasury headed by three senior monks, the under-cellarer, the receiver of money from Glastonbury barony, and the receiver of casual payments. There all money not assigned to a particular department should be paid. The archbishop's fears had probably been correct and his remedy proved the right one, though by the end of the Middle Ages the system seems to have been somewhat modified.

In 1414 Glastonbury's income in Somerset was valued for tax purposes, and the total of £1135 14s 6d was divided as follows:

Abbot	£935 1 10
Prior	£268

43 Seal of Stephen Wymborn, prior of Glastonbury, 1398

Sacristan	£59
Almoner	£50
Chamberlain	£35
Pittancer	£19 15 8
Kitchener	£19 3 4
Infirmarian	£6 2 8
Hosteler	£4
Precentor	£2 14 4
Gardener	£2 10 0

To those, of course, should at Glastonbury be added other office holders whose charges were met from the general funds or from the produce of their own departments: the sub-prior, the third prior, inner and foreign cellarers, the receivers or treasurer and the medar.

The title of each office holder gives some clue as to his duties. The prior, the abbot's right-hand man, had particular charge of the almshouse for widows near St Patrick's chapel, the sacristan was responsible for the abbey church, its services, vestments, ornaments and lights; the almoner for rather more than care for the poor, in which he was helped by a sub-almoner; the chamberlain produced clothing for each member of the community; the pittancer supplied extra food for the monks in Advent and Lent; the kitchener and the inner cellarer (sometimes called the cellarer of the hall) managed the food supply for monks and servants alike; the foreign cellarer had general oversight of the abbey estates and was sometimes called steward; the infirmarian for both the buildings and the sick in the infirmary; the hosteler was the guestmaster caring for visitors; the precentor paid for special services and especially for the chapel on top of the Tor; the gardener produced vegetables and herbs; and the medar dispensed mead and wine.

Smaller houses naturally had more modest arrangements and different names. At the election of Bishop Jocelin in 1206 all the Bath priory monks put their signatures and offices to a deed recording their votes. There were then 41 monks led by Robert the prior, and the officers comprised almoner, cellarer, chamberlain, clerk of works, granary-keeper, infirmarian, precentor, refectorer, sacrist, and treasurer, each heading a separate department within the house, with assistants for the prior (sub-prior and third prior), precentor and sacrist. Bishop Stillington, when formally visiting Bath in 1476, considered that the prior, the sub-prior, the sacristan and the precentor were the most influential members of the community and examined them personally. His officials were left to question the rest of the house, among whom were the chamberlain, the infirmarian, the succentor, the third prior and the kitchener.

Those monastic officials at Taunton who received direct cash rents to exercise their duties were naturally named in the sole surviving account roll dating from 1420 or a few years before. After the prior, Walter Duffeld the sacrist received the largest sum, followed by the infirmarian, an office in which in that

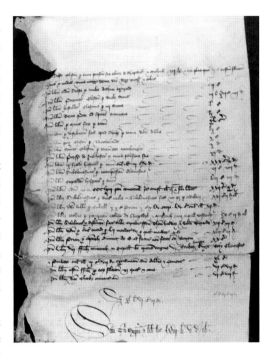

44 Glastonbury abbey: the almoner accounts for 2s paid to the Sacrist for 'cleaning the tomb of Arthur', 1446-7

year John Lymyn was followed by Thomas Yonge. Robert Nyweton was pittancer, Robert Gillyngham cellarer, Walter Leke cook, Peter Mede chamberlain and William Pole hosteler.

At Keynsham in 1526 the monastic officials were named as prior, sub-prior, sacrist, infirmarer, chancellor, cook and refectorer. As long ago as 1496 they had appointed a layman as their cellarer with a small cash salary and a generous allowance of convent ale each week. Bruton's obedientiaries in 1539 under the abbot were prior, sub-prior, chamberer (chamberlain), fermerer (infirmarer), cellarer, chaunter (precentor), steward, fraterer (kitchener) and chaplain. Muchelney in 1535 besides the abbot, prior and sub-prior were almoner, refectorer, precentor, sacristan, kitchener, chamberlain, keeper of the Lady Chapel and gatekeeper (both of whom had separate incomes for their duties), and a pittancer and a medar receiving income from the general abbey fund.

The men who managed these monastic departments became experts in their own fields just as choir monks were specialists. It was evidently unusual when Bishop Walter Haselshaw in 1308 allowed William le Pistor, canon of Bruton, to have a separate chamber, meals and allowances because of his industry and skill as cellarer, for the grant was made specifically because he had relieved the priory from a great burden of debt. Later such grants became more common. Robert Wynchestre of Athelney in 1401 received permission to keep the room he had been given for official purposes, and also to dispose of possessions he had acquired through his official duties. At Glastonbury the foreign cellarer and the receiver both necessarily spent time on the estates and their seats in choir were often vacant during the daily offices and the rooms where they kept accounts and met lay staff under their direction drew them inexorably away from community life. John Crosse probably held high administrative office at Glastonbury longer than any other: he was abbot's chaplain in 1350, receiver for 25 years from 1352 and then became prior. Walter Staunton had a similar record: receiver by 1392 until 1404 or later and foreign cellarer from 1408 until 1413 or later. Small wonder that men who had served like that were reluctant to give up the privileges which they had enjoyed. At the beginning of 1399 Richard Hounsworth, a Glastonbury monk, received papal permission to hold the office of chamberlain for life, on the grounds that his studies at Oxford had been interrupted when summoned back to hold 'divers and great offices' and because he was also 'aged and weak'. His claim was not entirely true, at least as regards his age and health for in 1408 he was well enough to hold the burdensome office of foreign cellarer and corrupt enough to be relieved of office and sent in disgrace to Hyde abbey. In 1445 both John Ledbury and John Codeworthe, respectively foreign cellarer and sacrist at Glastonbury were given the promise of their rooms and their food allowances for life on their retirement, though Codeworthe remained sacrist for another ten years and had the permission repeated.

Under these monk-officials each monastery according to its size had a necessary body of servants. In 1304 the prior and 26 monks at Montacute employed Geoffrey the gatekeeper, William the convent cook, Richard, who served in the infirmary, and John de Aula, whose name suggests he served in the monks' refectory. Glastonbury in 1322 had as many as 60 servants including porters, smiths, carters, cooks, millers, stablemen, a wheelwright, a hooper, brewers, grooms, and general servants in guesthouse, kitchen, cellar, gatehouses, almonry, refectory and infirmary. In 1361-2 there were 15 in the cellarer's office alone plus others hired including three maltsters, a washerwoman, two gardeners, three fishermen at Meare and two fence makers at Norwood. In 1455 the bishop told the abbot of Athelney to re-employ a barber and a tailor and when they had nothing else to do they were to help in the infirmary. Muchelney's servants in 1535 included a gardener, a laundress, a brewer, a barber and an eggman.

In the last full year of its life the community at Keynsham appointed a baker at 40s, a robe and pasture for a cow; and a brewer for 40s, four loaves a week and three flagons of ale, hay for his horse, a robe and a cow pasture. Among 12 other corrodians, together costing a total of nearly £39, were an usher and a marshall of the hall, a keeper of the bedchambers, a valet of the chamber, a doorkeeper, and a keeper of horses. The last account for Montacute for the year immediately before its dissolution included costs of servants and agricultural workers, cloth bought for domestic servants and necessary food given for workers on the home farm.

One special group of servants formerly attached to Witham and Hinton were different. The lay brethren of Carthusian houses worked the land and provided the food for men who seldom left their cells, let alone their cloister. They were, at the beginning, a recognised, celibate part of the community, though living at some distance from the great cloister.

By the early fourteenth century at least one Witham lay brother was no longer celibate. John Fisher agreed with the prior to work as a fisherman, plumber or at any other task he

45 The tomb of John Cammell (d.1487), St John's church, Glastonbury. Cammell was probably a lay official of the abbey

might be given, receiving in return, for himself and his wife a loaf, a flask of beer and a dish of pottage, the rations for a monk, together with a small sum in cash, two pairs of shoes, a pair of stockings, an old tunic and four shillings wages.

The lay brethren of both Witham and Hinton lived about a mile away from the monks, both settlements later known as Friary, to the confusion of many. Witham Friary has for long been the main settlement in the parish. By the mid-fifteenth century, however, the devotion of the people, according to the prior's petition, had waxed cold and there were no lay brethren, but instead 'secular persons of both sexes' were living there to work the monks' land. So Bishop Bekynton gave permission for the prior to provide a burial ground and a font for the needs of the growing community.

12 Endowments and investments

The founders of monasteries gave what they had to give: land ranging from whole manors to small fields; rights to pasture cattle on moors and in woods; churches, which at first meant the right to appoint parochial clergymen but came to mean some or all of the land attached to the church as well as tithes once given to support clergymen; and in the course of time houses in towns, rents, shares of church income called pensions or portions; and a whole range of properties such as fisheries, markets, fairs and other sources of income. From the manors and large estates came grain and meat, fish, wine and cider, and raw materials such as wool, hides, timber and stone. The cash from the sales of agricultural surpluses and raw materials paid artists, craftsmen and labourers, lawyers, administrators and politicians, and provided those items of food and drink not available at home like white fish from the north Atlantic and sweet wines of Spain and Portugal.

46 The George, Norton St Philip, a cloth warehouse for Hinton priory's fairs

Monastic estates

Only twice during the Middle Ages is it possible to get some idea of the property belonging to religious houses as a whole. In 1291 a survey was made by officials of Pope Nicholas IV which formed the basis for taxation for the next 200 years. **Table I** is a list of those Somerset monasteries recorded then and of the taxable values (not necessarily the full value) of their properties of all kinds first inside the county and then outside.

Table I: The possessions of Somerset houses in 1291

	Somerset	Elsewhere	Total
Athelney	£72 1s 4d	£6 13s 4d	£78 14s 4d
Barlinch	£8 3s 4d	£2 10s 0d	£10 13s 4d
Barrow	£1 6s 8d	£1 6s 8d	
Bath	£66 17s 7d★	£24 0s 8d	£90 18s 3d
Bridgwater, St John's	?	£10 13s 4d	?
Bruton	£33 13s 4d		£33 13s 4d
Cannington	?	13s 4d	?
Cleeve	£16 4s 6d	£28 12s 2d	£44 16s 8d
Dunster	£19 0s 7d		£19 0s 7d
Glastonbury	£1020 11s 8d	£382 11s 8d	£1403 3s 4d
Hinton	£68 9s 3d		£68 9s 3d
Keynsham	£68 9s 4d	£13 15s 4d	£82 4s 8d
Montacute	£163 6s 1d	£9 13s 6d	£173 19s 7d
Muchelney	£38 8s 6d		£38 8s 6d
Stogursey	£34 19s 6d		£34 19s 6d
Taunton	£27 4s 11d	£4 17s 9d	£32 2s 8d
Witham	£30 0s 0d		£30 0s 0d
Woodspring	£4 15s 0d		£4 15s 0d

★Includes £2 10s shared with Bermondsey (Surrey)

The second survey of monastic property, the *Valor Ecclesiasticus*, was made by order of King Henry VIII in 1535 and seems to have been more accurate. However, there are some serious gaps in the surviving record. **Table II** shows, as accurately as possible, the net income of each Somerset house, this time in descending order of size.

Table II: Net income of Somerset monasteries, 1535

	over £
Glastonbury	3311
Bath	617
Montacute	456
Muchelney	447
Bruton	439
Keynsham	419
Taunton	286
Hinton	248
Buckland	223
Witham	215
Athelney	209
Cleeve	155
Templecombe	107
Buckland (hospitallers)	103
Barlinch	98
Woodspring	91
Cannington	39
Dunster	37
Barrow Gurney	24

Note: Missing from this list are the friars and hospitals, omitted from the survey, and Burtle, Stavordale and Stogursey which had been taken over or closed before 1535 (see Gazetteer)

This is not the place to study in detail the way in which each monastery exploited its estates from its foundation until the end of the religious life in Henry VIII's reign. Only for Glastonbury might that be possible, for the records of other houses do not survive beyond a few stray account or rent rolls. Some overall picture, however, ought to be attempted to illustrate the different kinds of income monasteries enjoyed, not simply from direct farming but also from rents and tithes.

Domesday Book records the distinct ways in which monasteries exploited their land in Somerset. Bath cathedral priory had 15 separate holdings in the county, beginning with the borough of Bath itself, where 24 burgesses paid rent of 20s, a water mill on the Avon was worth the same and there was a meadow beside the river. Then there were nine estates, such as Priston, Stanton Prior and Bathford, held 'in demesne', that is directly,

47 The house assigned to the vicar of Muchelney by the abbot 1308. The fine window in the hall dates from the fifteenth century

small parts held by villagers in return for their labour on the main farm, the produce from which would have been sent to the monks or sold. And there were five estates whose main farms were held by laymen such as Walter Hussey, who occupied farms at Wilmington, Charlcombe and Batheaston.

The pattern, on a smaller scale, was different on the estates of Muchelney and Athelney. Muchelney owned directly all its Somerset estates beginning with the three islands in the marshes south of Langport called Muchelney, which meant 'great island', Midelney and Thorney, and including Drayton, Ilminster, Isle Abbots and West Camel. Athelney owned Seavington and Hamp directly and entirely and its other properties were shared with some of the country's largest landowners like the king's half-brother, the count of Mortain, who held parts of Ilton and Ashill.

Glastonbury, the only other Somerset monastery whose lands were surveyed in Domesday Book, also held many estates directly and many more were let to tenants, who in course of time became virtual owners. The 'home' estate of Glastonbury had three associated islands and included fisheries, vineyards, woodland and a good deal of meadow and pasture; and somewhere, presumably in the town, eight smiths were at work. Elsewhere on this vast holding could be found mills and an army of villagers, cottagers and serfs. The estate at Ham, for instance, represented now by the parish of High Ham, comprised a large 'home' farm with five serfs, smaller estates held by three lay tenants with four serfs, and the rest of the land farmed in differing amounts by 59 peasants.

In 1086 Abbot Thurstan reported to the king that there were on his 'home' farm at Ham two horses, 17 cattle, 10 pigs and 150 sheep. Nearly a hundred years later, in 1171, there were 28 cattle including 16 oxen for ploughing and 10 cows for butter and cheese; and the peasants paid cash rents and honey as well as giving labour on the abbot's farm. By 1198 the rents had risen from 73s 4d to 110s 9d.

A careful study of the surviving accounts of the abbey manor at High Ham would reveal the pattern of tenant farms and farming activities over the next three centuries, and would indicate when the abbey ceased to take grain or meat or wool from their manor and took only cash rents. When in 1515 Thomas Sutton, the abbey foreign cellarer, came to visit the estate as part of his great survey for Abbot Bere he found that the home farm was occupied by William Balche who was described as 'farmer', that is a man put in to work the land for his own profit but paying only a rent equal to a nominal valuation. The farm comprised a barn, an oxshed and a yard, a 10-acre wood containing 112 oak trees, 38½ acres of grassland divided into several small fields, and 188 acres of arable strips scattered in the village's two open fields. For the entire farm he paid rent of £4 13s 4d. A few years later Balche was given notice to quit and the farm was divided between several tenants, men who already held land there from the abbey. Those men, whose names are not recorded, paid a realistic rent more than £5 above what Balche had paid.

The abbey had one other source of income from High Ham, the tithes of grain paid by all its tenant farmers. That grain, it was still remembered in the later sixteenth century, was taken to Glastonbury from the parsonage barn 'by boats and litters through a ditch made by hand for that purpose'; the ditch, one of many crossing the marshes of the Levels and known as Hardenes ditche, was still then recognisable.

The canons of Bruton had an estate called the rectory of South Petherton. They had held it since 1181-2 and it comprised some land and the tithes of grain and hay paid throughout the ancient parish which included Barrington, Chillington, Stratton, Lopen, Drayton, Compton, Wigborough and also, for convenience of collection by 1514, from Swell and Upton. John Brett, a man of prominence in Petherton, was acting by 1511 as the canons' bailiff and in the year 1514-15 paid them over £48 for the tithes. Rents from land, sales of beans, wheat, hens and chickens paid instead of cash, the tithes of mills and fines levied in the four annual courts produced in that year a grand total income of over £71. The costs for the year were small: 5s for repairing the chancel at Chillington, 5s 4d for carrying stone from Ham Hill when the great barn was being built; charges for giving bread to 11 tenants on Christmas Eve and for the archdeacon of Taunton's fees. In fact £53 was handed over to Richard Bishop, the canons' receiver-general; but all was not well. John Brett himself paid over very little of his rent and the total arrears going back 25 years amounted to the huge sum of over £157. Eight years later the arrears still amounted to over £132.

The monks of Athelney had owned Long Sutton since King Alfred's time and at Domesday their home farm there amounted to about half the parish. In 1349 it measured 132 acres, mostly of arable land, and was still farmed for the monks. Probably not long after that, when agricultural labour to run the farm became expensive, it was easier and more sensible to find a tenant to pay cash rent. From 1537 Robert Golde rented the home farm, including the abbot's manor house with its hall, kitchen, buttery, brewhouse and

*48 Athelney abbey:
account roll for
Ilton, 1459-60*

three bedchambers with 145 acres of arable land and some grassland for a total of £14 a year. That was just one part of the estate. Another was the rectory, including the tithe of all the grain grown: in 1538, 60 quarters of wheat and eight quarters of dredge corn were sold, six quarters of wheat and six quarters of dredge were given to the vicar of the parish.

The way monasteries exploited land changed radically between the later eleventh century when Domesday Book was compiled and the Dissolution. From direct farmers of the estates monasteries had become largely *rentiers*, landlords receiving mostly cash instead of labour and produce. During that period of four-and-a-half centuries many houses, directly or indirectly, had been pioneers, draining the low-lying marshes to create high quality grassland, running huge flocks of sheep and breeding dairy cows and riding horses. They and their tenants had been growers of grain, producers of cheese, butter, wine (until the climate proved unsuitable), cider, leather, withies, thatching reed, timber and more.

From the abbey's estates in 1361-2 the Glastonbury granger received wheat, barley and oats from most of the directly farmed manors in Somerset and from three in Dorset, Sturminster Newton, Marnhull and Buckland Newton, but none from Wiltshire manors. The total of grain was over 2,800 quarters, the most productive manors being Zoy, Podimore, Ditcheat, Doulting and Brent, now nearly all grass. Other supplies coming into the barn were mixtures of beans and wheat, beans and pulse, rye and wheat. Some of the grain was turned into malt for brewing; most of the best wheat passed to the monastic baker, some went straight to the kitchen, more for horse fodder, smaller amounts to the kitchener, the pittancer, the infirmarer, the chamberlain and the gardener.

In the mid-fifteenth century the monks at Muchelney still raised their own stock. They began the year 1439-40 with one bull, 19 cows, 13 steers, 11 heifers and 18 calves. During the year a cow proved sterile and two calves were slaughtered and delivered to the monastery kitchen. They also had five stallions, two of which were brought into the abbot's stable and two sold, and 13 mares, five yearlings, and seven colts and foals.

49 Abbot William Dovell of Cleeve (1507-36) agrees to lease some land to a member of the Luttrell family

Sheep, those flexible animals which could flourish on the Levels in summer and could survive harsh winters on the Mendips or Exmoor, were vital to the larger communities, though as usual only Glastonbury's records are full enough to offer some idea of their importance. They produced milk, wool, meat and, perhaps most important, manure. In 1330 the abbot had flocks at Doulting, Wrington, Marksbury, Batcombe and Pilton, a combined total of 1,504 beasts. Better conditions on the Levels later in the fourteenth century allowed a successful flock of 222 wethers at Street in 1365-6 and over 200 at Walton in the 1390s. In the next century the Mells flock on Mendip was over 300 strong, the Carthusians of Hinton had a flock of 1,000 not far away, and the Witham Carthusians in 1539 handed over their grange at Charterhouse Hidon where 100 ewes were pastured.

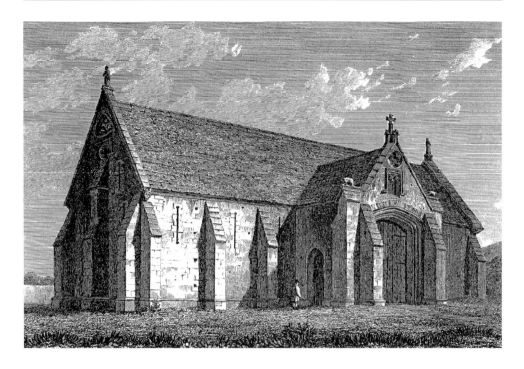

50 Glastonbury abbey: the barn at Glastonbury

In the years of financial crisis just before the Dissolution sheep took on another value; they became negotiable assets. In 1532 the abbot of Cleeve needed £200 so he handed over his entire flock of 1,200 wethers and 200 ewes to Richard Smyth alias Brampson, a vicar choral of Wells cathedral and already financially involved with St John's hospital at Wells. The abbot was to lease them back for five years, during which time he agreed to pay Smyth half the profits from the wool and lambs, some £12 13s 4d a year, and at the end of the lease to return the entire flock to the value of £108. Smyth's terms seem to have been somewhat harsh, but his caution was not misplaced: the sheep were not handed back, for by the end of the lease Cleeve abbey had been closed. Smyth was eventually awarded £120 in compensation. The descendants of Cleeve's flock no doubt wandered on the Brendons under other ownership.

The prior of Bath had flocks on the hills around the city in some places where sheep have not grazed for centuries. In 1534-5 he had a herd of hogs at Lyncombe which he leased to a farmer named Robert Cokkes for a term of 70 years. Three years later the prior leased the rest of the priory's sheep to two other farmers, 80 ewes on Lansdown to Richard Chapman and 280 wethers at South Stoke to Thomas Smith and his wife. During the same years the other farms on the priory's estate at Bathford, Combe and Lyncombe were also leased. All leases were long, offering a substantial sum for the priory at the beginning but only a modest annual rent. Was Prior Bird trying to preserve the convent's property from what he perceived to be some threat of taxation, or simply looking for immediate cash from entry fines and sympathetic neighbours?

By the end of the Middle Ages Bruton's estate at South Petherton, like very many monastic properties, was being treated simply as a source of cash, no longer of produce in kind. In 1511-12, for example, most of the land was let to men whose predecessors had once been obliged by law to work on the canons' home farm, ploughing, sowing, reaping, mowing, stacking, cutting, threshing and winnowing the hay or grain, while labourers had been paid directly to care for the sheep flock or the dairy and to see that eggs and poultry, fish, meat and cheese found their way to the canons' kitchen. Now in 1511-12 only cash found its way to Bruton: £48 10s from rents of that home farm whose acres spread from South Petherton itself into Bridge, Drayton, Wigborough, Stratton, Chillington, Lopen, Upton and Barrington. Nearly £18 came from rents from the small holdings of those former labouring tenants; 30s from tithes including the tithes of two water mills; just over 21s from the sale of rents of hens, chickens, wheat or beans; and 5s 3d from fines paid to the manor court.

The monastic landscape

The survival of so few accounts of Somerset monastic manors beyond those of Glastonbury makes any kind of summary of the development of the agricultural policy and methods of religious houses impossible. Yet there are clues in the landscape of the Levels, where Glastonbury lands marched with those of Athelney and Muchelney, which strongly suggest that where Glastonbury led others followed, sometimes with an ill grace.

Current opinion, for instance, is inclined to the view that the regular grid pattern of the villages on the north side of the Poldens, at Chilton Polden, Edington, Catcott and Shapwick in particular, may be the result of deliberate policy, nothing less than a wholesale reorganisation of settlement. The removal of the church of Shapwick from its ancient position to the centre of the village in 1331-2 was but the end of a process which had been taking place quite noticeably for half a century, and probably more gradually for much longer. Planned settlement may also be seen at Newtown in West Pennard, where 'new place' was mentioned in the late twelfth century, the Newtown of a century later.

The creation of towns may also in some cases have been deliberate policy. Glastonbury's street pattern is, quite obviously, governed by the position of the abbey precinct; the earliest reference to St John's church includes the name Northbin, that site to the north of the monastic enclosure. Middle Street, the Borough and South Street, all part of the road through Montacute, were deliberately built up, the Borough *c*.1100, the rest in the thirteenth century, to create a small town and thus to provide the monks with a better income than was to be expected from agricultural tenants alone.

Bruton and Keynsham abbeys both stand apart from the little towns which grew up, presumably with their encouragement, around the sites of markets; Taunton priory was deliberately placed outside the town's defences on a new site when the older, too near the castle, had for the convenience of both to be moved. Bridgwater's hospital, like the similar hospitals at Taunton, Wells, and those in Bath and Bristol suburbs were so placed because of their special function, offering hospitality to travellers and those whom society perhaps shunned. The friaries at Bridgwater and Ilchester were, by contrast, as

51 The site of the monastery at Bruton in the eighteenth century

near to the centre of urban business as possible, their sites squeezed into an existing street pattern.

In the countryside monastic sites might be more or less transforming. Muchelney, Athelney and Burtle were by design confined to their islands, their buildings to be seen and their bells heard across moor and marsh. The adjoining island at Muchelney became the site of a settlement and Athelney's nearest neighbour across the Baltmoor Wall was the old Saxon fortress of Lyng. Burtle remained isolated until the end. Barlinch, too, had no near neighbours in its Exmoor valley, but Cleeve, whose Cistercian purpose had been to settle in loneliness, by design or accident peopled the flowery valley with granges and successfully cultivated the steep slopes, holding even the vicious broom at bay.

In the Levels, monastic ownership has left clear traces. Glastonbury, and to a lesser extent Muchelney and Athelney, along with the canons of Wells cathedral were pioneer drainage engineers involved in straightening rivers, creating new watercourses, building protective embankments, causeways and sea walls. It was not, of course, a question of improvement for the public good, rather of exploitation to maximise the produce of the land, but tenants as well and landlords benefited.

Many of the improvements are impossible to date exactly, but remarkable engineering feats were somehow achieved. The construction of the Baltmoor Wall *c.*1154 cut the West Yeo river and forced what became the Tone to flow south of Athelney to join the Parrett at Burrow Mump, thus protecting the grasslands to the north. Burrow Wall, east of the same Mump, kept the swollen waters of the Cary from overflowing into the Glastonbury grasslands of Othery and Middlezoy — and incidentally forced them into the territory of

52 The island site of Atheney abbey

the lay landlord of Aller. The course of the Brue north of the Poldens was undoubtedly straightened and its flow improved, to the vast benefit of many but by no means least the lands of Glastonbury around Brent Knoll.

Beer Wall, Lake Wall, Fountains Wall, Greylake Fosse, Mark Causeway and many much smaller earthworks, often traceable in the landscape by their regularity, as well as the early fourteenth-century Pillrow Cut and other examples of canalisation tell the story of piecemeal drainage beyond the immediate confines of established villages. Tenant farmers, encouraged by favourable rents, dug ditches around previously flooded grassland plots, thus extending the area of improved ground further and further into the marsh. The once relatively small watery island of Zoy became during the course of the thirteenth century an enormously extended and prosperous triple community, three large and prosperous villages of Weston Zoyland, Middlezoy and Othery in place of one core village and two hamlets all ignored by the compilers of Domesday Book.

The larger ditches or rhines had a secondary purpose, as means of communication. Some time before the 1240s a Glastonbury tenant named Robert Malherbe had responsibility for almost the entire communications network of central Somerset. He had to provide a boat crewed by eight men and large enough to carry the abbot, his men, his kitchen equipment, his huntsmen and his dogs almost the entire length of the Brue from Pilton to Brent. He was also responsible for the delivery of messages from various places on the river bank inland, for carrying wine to Glastonbury from the vineyards at Pilton and Panborough, for taking the abbey cellarer on fishing trips to Meare, for guarding the fisheries as far as Clewer and Mark, for keeping Hertymoor in West Pennard and for maintaining the abbot's boats.

It was still remembered in the later years of the sixteenth century that grain from the Glastonbury estate at High Ham was taken by boats from the parish across Sedgemoor 'through a dytch made by hand for that purpose w[hi]ch ditch at this day they commonly call Hardenes ditche, whereof is yet manifest signe to be seene'. That was probably the Harding's Ditch mentioned in 1280. Exactly how it reached the abbey is something of a mystery.

One other form of investment combined the product of sheep with the power of water. Fulling mills may in a physical sense have been relatively insignificant in the landscape, often hidden deep in river valleys, but their part in the production of Somerset cloth was crucial. Fast-running streams of the Brendons and the Quantocks drove a mill for Cleeve near Washford in the 1240s and for Taunton priory at Thurloxton by the earlier fifteenth century. Similar small but fast-flowing brooks running from the north into Bruton drove mills for both Bruton and Stavordale. Abbot Bere built one at Northover, on the more sluggish Brue between Glastonbury and Street, at the turn of the sixteenth century. Keynsham was perhaps more enterprising than the rest. It had at least three fulling mills by 1487 and another by 1495 in the valleys of the Chew and the Avon.

Cloth from Somerset sheep was mostly sent out of the county through Bridgwater, Bristol and perhaps some of the southern ports by collecting and selling agents whose names and activities are hardly known. One of the important points of sale was Norton St Philip, where the George Inn was built by the Hinton Carthusians in the late fourteenth century and refronted in the 1430s. In the 1530s and undoubtedly earlier the guestrooms became storage space for the linen cloth offered for sale at the great April fair. The market crosses at Bruton and Glastonbury, the first built by Abbot Elye probably in the 1530s, the other perhaps by Abbot Bere at the turn of the century, marked just two more trading places to be found across the county. Both succumbed to the demands of traffic in the early nineteenth century.

Barns, preserved because they proved so useful to later farmers, still declare the importance of farming. Their opposing porches provided the space and the draught for threshing floors, while their ample bays kept dry all manner of produce, grown on demesne farm or paid as rent in kind or tithe.

Half a century and more after the Dissolution, witnesses in disputes heard in the Court of Exchequer on questions of rights to tithe recalled graphic details of what was even then an almost forgotten way of life. One remembered seeing Cleeve monks, each wearing a new pair of gloves, pulling up young broom plants until their gloves were well worn and their hands sore. Another, a butcher of about 90 years, looked back in 1609 to when he was a teenager 'attending and waiting on a monk of the same house . . . did often times go into the said South Field when the abbot's own ploughman did plough the arable lands there'. Both recollections were, so they appear, entirely neutral. The collective memory of the people of High Ham, passed on to their rector and recorded by him in the 1570s was of exploitation on a grand scale as well as gross spiritual neglect. The neglect can be proved to be quite unfounded, the exploitation difficult to demonstrate one way or the other, though it is perhaps worth recording that the farmers of High Ham were content to retain the essential elements of the ancient system of open-field cultivation for another three centuries.

13 Dissolution, dispersal and dispossession

The end of a thousand years of religious community life, while actually achieved by parliamentary decision on Crown initiative, was marked by remarkably little evidence of public outrage, however much private distress may have been caused. Claims of scandalous behaviour, incompetence or simply a relaxation of standards were by no means new in the sixteenth century. The life of the religious had not been designed to be easy, and almost from the beginning the involvement of the secular world had forced compromises upon men and women whose pure intent thus came under pressure. Only those houses of strict observance such as the Carthusians at Hinton and Witham in Somerset and elsewhere, the Bridgettines of Syon and the Observant friars were recognised by their contemporaries as religious worthy of the name, but even they sank with the rest, inspiring in the martyrdom of some of their number.

For a century and more the Augustinian Order had been concerned about a fall in their standard of devotion. In 1434 a decree from one of their General Chapters complained of the idleness and ignorance of novices, and in 1518 someone spoke of the 'lamentable ruin of all monasticism that is imminent'. Injunctions drawn up after a visitation of Barlinch in 1509 reflected a malaise which was evidently universal. Nothing was dreadfully bad, but if canons were leaving the house without permission, were eating meals alone and not listening to edifying reading while eating, were employing more than one servant each, were not keeping monastic silence, were contradicting their seniors, were not employing a grammar teacher, were not keeping the dormitory in repair, and were not maintaining a light in their church, then they were falling very short of their Rule.

The infiltration of the world

The Carthusians, from the very beginning of their Order, had realised that the only way they could live entirely withdrawn from the world was to employ a regular body of servants (*conversi*) to work their estates, produce their food and clothing and maintain their buildings. Even then one of their number in each house, like St Hugh at La Grande Chartreuse, acted as administrator or procurator.

The abbot of a large Benedictine house like Glastonbury, by contrast, found himself personally standing beside secular landlords exercising secular rights and duties. In fact the abbot of Glastonbury was, by virtue of the vast estates of his house, a lord of Parliament with national if not international responsibilities. What effect such external interests of their abbot had on his community can only be guessed at; the surviving kitchen and the outlines of the impressive hall are tangible evidence of the abbot's role in the secular society of Somerset.

That role may in some instances have been only nominal: the abbot stood beside the bishop of Bath and Wells as the leading ecclesiastic in the county and well above most secular landowners. Both found themselves appointed to commissions of the peace, drainage commissions and enquiries into all manner of local issues such as in 1367 the precise boundary between Somerset and Devon and in 1373 the boundary of the new county of Bristol. And Glastonbury, as the largest taxpayer, was often involved either in tax and subsidy assessment or collection or both and in 1360, for instance, was required to accept the total tax from the county on deposit. Only after 1441, thanks to some special pleading about the problems of flooding and to the diplomatic work of Abbot Nicholas Frome, was Glastonbury exempted from collecting within the diocese. The other houses were obliged to continue the unwelcome task.

Abbot John Chinnock of Glastonbury found himself in 1399 on a commission to declare Richard II deposed and two of his successors were sent on embassies abroad; duties far removed from those which they might have expected as novices, but entirely consonant with those of the head of a vast estate. And, similarly, whenever the Crown had a financial crisis Glastonbury was among many monasteries which provided cash and hoped to be repaid from taxation later. So, for instance, in 1347 for the expedition to France which culminated in the victory at Crecy, Glastonbury produced £60, in 1359 300 marks (£200), in 1377, 1379 and 1386 £100 and in 1395 and 1397 500 marks (£333 6s 8d). In 1522 Abbot Bere lent the king £1,000 for his personal expenses in France. Other Somerset houses could afford much less, but between 1347 and 1397 Bruton, Athelney, Muchelney, Bath, Keynsham and Taunton, in that order, contributed in loans a total of £407. And unlike Glastonbury, those houses continued to act as collectors of clerical taxes until the Dissolution, a responsibility which involved employing collectors and agents to deal on their behalf with the king's Exchequer, just another distraction from a life of prayer and contemplation.

Finance, of course, was hardly a worry at Glastonbury although in earlier days Abbot Roger thought it prudent in 1259 to seek the pope's permission to borrow 1,532 marks (£1,021 6s 8d) to meet his expenses when he went to Rome. Two centuries later, when Abbot Nicholas Frome was preparing to attend the Council of Basle, he asked the king for licence to export 100 marks worth of gold and silver.

The abbot of Glastonbury was obviously in a position to be banker to friends and neighbours, and on occasion may have been a reluctant lender. John Selwood and Richard Bere put money into church buildings. Selwood provided cash in the 1470s when High Ham church was being rebuilt and probably also helped to finance church building at Meare, Weston Zoyland and Ditcheat, where his initials are still to be seen. Bere presumably gave some money when Bruton parish church was being enlarged, since his shield along with those of Abbot Gilbert of Bruton and Richard FitzJames, bishop of London and a native of the parish, are to be seen on the crenellations of the north clerestory.

Dame Elizabeth FitzJames, who had a house in the Glastonbury hamlet of Wick, deposited some plate with Abbot Whiting at the request of her husband in exchange for

53 Initials of Abbot Richard Bere of Glastonbury (1493-1525) from the church of St Benignus, Glastonbury

£20 cash for use in London. John Lyte borrowed £40 in 1537 from Abbot Whiting to pay for building work at his home. He repaid £10 early in 1539 but the abbot pressed for the rest and took Lyte to law. At the end of June the rest was found and delivered to Whiting in his garden while mass was being sung in the abbey church. Eight nobles were returned on condition that Lyte put the abbot's coat-of-arms on the building. John Walton of Low Ham borrowed from Abbot Whiting and repaid £10 on 24 June 1539.

Helping friends and neighbours was one thing; taking risks under pressure from the mighty was another. Abbot Selwood acted as banker for two desperate politicians. He lent Humphrey Stafford, earl of Devon, 500 marks (£333 6s 8d) and on the latter's summary execution at Bridgwater in 1469 permitted him to be buried under one of the arches on the south side of the nave. Some £33 of the loan was repaid in cash by Stafford's executor in April 1470 and silver-gilt plate — two flagons and two salt cellars weighing 178oz and valued at over £269 — in July. Whether the rest was repaid is unknown.

Very soon afterwards Abbot Selwood took custody of a gold cup, a little gold salt cellar, a portnos and a locked casket 'stuffyd' with jewels and other things left with him by Lord Wenlock, one of Queen Margaret of Anjou's commanders, when he arrived on a recruiting march through the county a few days before the battle of Tewkesbury in May

54 Lady FitzJames borrows cash from the abbot of Glastonbury

55 Abbot Richard Whiting lends John Walton of Netherham £10, 1539

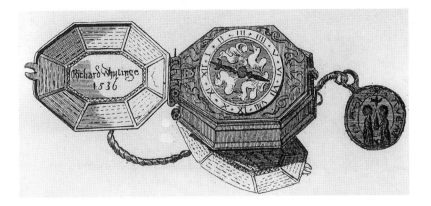

56 Abbot Whiting's watch and seal

1471. After Wenlock's death there the abbot was in some danger of being accused of supporting traitors and was no doubt glad to hand the valuables over to Wenlock's widow, being careful to take out a substantial bond from her to cover any risk.

Abbot Bere probably had little choice but to lend the duke of Buckingham £333 6s 8d, and perhaps did not hold much store by the duke's promise to repay by instalments beginning at Christmas 1518. In 1522 the abbot of St Albans borrowed £40 and by the end of his rule Bere had lent as much as £2,809 to such people as Stephen Gardiner, bishop elect of Winchester, Hugh Inge, archbishop elect of Dublin, Chief Justice Sir John FitzJames and his wife Elizabeth, the prior of Barnstaple, Lord Sandes of the Vyne and a group of local clergy, merchants and local gentlemen.

For other communities, debts rather than loans or gifts were far more common. In the last full year of life Montacute priory's financial burdens were heavy, and while the pensions paid were almost entirely in support of religious activities, the fees reveal a very different picture. Some, of course, involved the administration of their estates — to the chief steward, auditors, under-stewards and bailiffs. Others show just how far monasteries were at the mercy of politicians and lawyers. The largest, £4, was paid to the Lord Privy Seal, Thomas Cromwell, Baron Cromwell, the king's vice-gerent in spirituals and architect of the destruction of the monasteries. And later on in the list were the sheriff and the escheator, the king's local officials, Sir Giles Strangways and Henry Strangways, members of a prominent local family, and two lawyers, all with local connections. The total cost in fees was £28 6s.

Nor was this situation unique. Fees paid by the monks of Muchelney amounted to £31 3s 4d headed by £4 to Cromwell, £2 to Sir John Tregonwell, one of the king's agents for the Dissolution, the sheriff and the escheator, the abbey's steward, under-steward and auditor, several other local gentry and three lawyers. Common to both, apart from Cromwell, were Sir John Horsey the steward, John Cuffe the auditor, and William Portman and Giles Penny the lawyers.

Athelney was in an equally parlous financial plight. Abbot John Major in 1531 bought on credit three decorated woven woollen floor coverings from an international cloth dealer for £13 6s 8d. His successor Robert Hamlyn admitted in 1533 that he personally owed 200 marks (£133 6s 8d) to Thomas Cromwell and that the community was in debt for over 1,500 marks (£1,000). He offered to pay it off in seven years, even if it meant

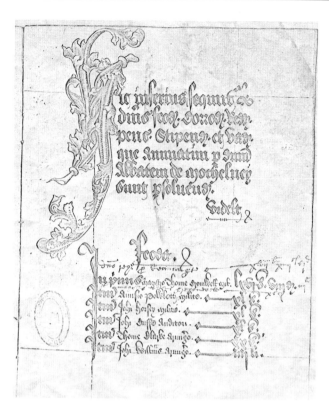

57 *Pensions and other charges owed by Muchelney abbey in the 1530s*

58 *The seal of Athelney abbey, used when the house surrendered in 1539*

himself eating bread and water two days a week. In 1536, evidently in spite of his promise and his efforts, there were debts of over £904, partly to those who had advanced money for Hamlyn's inevitable charges when he became abbot, partly the charges of employing servants to run the abbey estate and clergy to minster in the abbey's parishes. But how did a monastery come to owe cash to a furrier, a saddler and to merchants from Bridgwater, Bristol, Poole and even London?

In the event Athelney somehow held out until early in 1539 although Muchelney had closed quietly the year before. Hamlyn somehow could not bring himself to hand over his house to Lord Audley, who had the notion that it would make him a suitable dwelling.

The idea of suppression

The closure of or change to a religious house was not new, though admittedly uncommon; the majority provided a remarkably secure home for generations of religious but a few, the Templars for political reasons and some others because of changes within their Order, because they could no longer support a community or had radically changed their purpose, faced either closure or internal alteration.

59 Minchin Buckland: inventory of the preceptory, 1540

One of the earliest closures was the most radical. William Raven of the preceptory at Templecombe was the first Templar to be tried in London in 1309 after Pope Clement IV had demanded the arrest of all members of the Order. The Order was suppressed in 1312 and its members dispersed, and four other former members of Templecombe were sentenced to imprisonment for life at Muchelney, Taunton, Montacute and Glastonbury.

The alien priory of Stogursey was a community of only four in 1328 and by the end of the century had probably been reduced to a prior only. Its alien status had always made it vulnerable and by 1438 its estates were permanently in the hands of the Crown. Two years later they had been handed over to Eton college and the last prior left in 1442. The alien house at Yenston had disappeared much earlier, near the beginning of the Hundred Years War, the last prior mentioned in 1347. Houses at Buckland and Ilchester changed in character. Buckland was originally a house of Augustinian canons which became a preceptory of the Hospitallers and the home of all the sisters of the Order. At Ilchester a hospital run by a community of men and women changed in the later thirteenth century to be a convent for women only, but by 1423 there were only two nuns and a few years later it was a free chapel under a chaplain.

One other house, Stavordale, had also ceased to have an independent existence in 1533 when it was united with Taunton, a house of the same Order. For that reason, although small, it was not closed in 1536 but fell early in February 1539 as part of Taunton.

The Dissolution

Those later changes affected but a few and were hardly radical, and the suppression of Stogursey in favour of Eton was paralleled in many other parts of the country by closures organised by several bishops for the benefit of colleges at Oxford and Cambridge several years before Wolsey arranged the dissolution of St Frideswide's in Oxford to make way for Cardinal college and the closure of about 20 more for the same purpose. Further schemes never came to fruition because of Wolsey's fall, but by 1533 there was talk of general suppression and a year later a scheme to give religious a fixed income, to close monasteries of less than 13 monks, and to pass all surplus revenues to the king. A year later still and the appearance of the *Valor Ecclesiasticus* gave the government a detailed record of the value of monastic property, information which allowed those intent on suppression rather than reform to act with such speed and thoroughness. A judicial visitation of religious houses in the name of the king by clearly unsympathetic lay commissioners beginning in August 1535 was followed before their work was completed by the Act of Suppression in 1536 which demanded the surrender of all houses 'not . . . above the clear yearly value of two hundred pounds'. There was talk in the preamble of the Act of 'manifest sin, vicious, carnal, and abominable living' among such small houses and of religion 'right well kept and observed' in the larger houses whence, by implication, the dispossessed might go.

Three monks left Cleeve when it was closed in 1536 and joined Dunkeswell, one went to Newenham, both larger Devon houses of the same order, and found what they must have presumed were secure homes. Other Cleeve monks may have found homes at Forde or Buckland, but no pension lists for those have survived. Four men at least clung to the

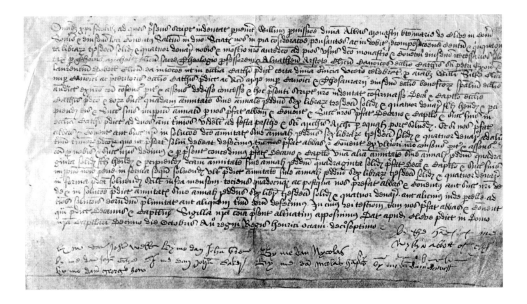

60 The community at Cleeve record their names, 1525

life they knew. One more, John Hooper, became a secular, was later appointed bishop of Gloucester, and subsequently bishop of Worcester and Gloucester, but in 1554 was deprived and in 1555 was burnt.

A similar story of transfer may be told of members of other small houses: Thomas Mathewe of Barlinch went to Taunton and William Brente *alias* Dunne and John Partriche of Woodspring to Keynsham in 1536, both again remaining Augustinian canons. Two nuns of Cannington had to leave the diocese when their house closed in 1536 for Barrow was closed, too; one went to Shaftesbury, one to Polsloe.

The closure of the small houses was the beginning of the end although in the next year or two there were, curiously, a few new foundations elsewhere in the country. There was much talk, too, of closures of larger houses, of voluntary surrenders, and clear action against the friars. The Franciscans of Bridgwater were suppressed in February 1538 (the Dominicans of Ilchester may have closed already) and Muchelney had already gone, apparently ready to give up even before the arrival of Cromwell's agent Thomas Legh. In the early months of 1539 the king's visitors moved swiftly from house to house, at each in a matter of days accepting surrender, arranging pensions and the sale or transfer of valuable assets. Keynsham and Bath closed in late January; Athelney, Bridgwater hospital, Buckland, Taunton and Wells hospital before the middle of February; Witham, Montacute, and Hinton in the second half of March; Bruton on the first day of April. Thus by the Spring of 1539 only one house in Somerset was open — Glastonbury.

It remained open until late September when the king's commissioners, having sent Abbot Whiting to the Tower and two other monks and two laymen to gaol locally, sent the rest of the community away. 'Very glad to depart', they told Cromwell. Surely not all of them.

The end of Glastonbury, as the end of Colchester and Reading, brought the tragedy of execution. Richard Whiting, John Arthur *alias* Thorne and Roger Wilffryde *alias* James were hanged on the Tor on 15 November 1539.

Financial recompense

Even allowing for the loss of sources, the disparity of treatment between heads of houses and other members of each community, and between men and women is difficult to explain. An abbot or prior willing to go without fuss might evidently negotiate a comfortable future and might well augment it with a cash gratuity or a house. Thus the abbot of Keynsham and the prior of Taunton each received a pension of £60 a year, their seconds-in-command £9 and £10 respectively, perhaps because of a disparity in age or education, the next two seniors £6 13s 4d and £6 each. After them at Taunton were eight canons each receiving the basic £5 6s 8d although Thomas Dale received a further £2 13s 4d for serving the cure of St James's church. John Fowler at Keynsham was one of five to receive the basic £5 6s 8d but with an additional £1 16s 8d for saying mass every holy day at St Margaret's, Queen Charlton. John Partriche and William Brente or Dunne were given only £5 and £4 13s 4d respectively; they had been turned out of Woodspring and may well have received some small pension then.

Most of the canons of Bruton similarly received the basic £5 6s 8d with an additional 13s 4d for their education, but why should Abbot John Elye have been awarded a pension of £80 and a gratuity of £20; and why should most of the monks of Montacute have £6 13s 4d and Prior Robert Whitlocke have £80 and the house he had recently built at East Chinnock? Most of the monks of Bath had the basic £5 6s 8d, too, with Prior William Holloway also having £80 and a house in the city worth a further 20s a year. Abbot Robert Hamlyn of Athelney had £50 and his prebend of Long Sutton in Wells cathedral, Abbot William Dovell of Cleeve £26 13s 4d.

It is understandable that the members of smaller houses received smaller pensions: Prior John Mychell of Witham £33 6s 8d, the master of St John's in Bridgwater £33 6s 8d (and a gratuity of £16 13s 4d) and his fellow of St John's in Wells £12. John Barwyke, the prior of Barlinch, received a pension of £13 6s 8d and a gratuity of the same sum. The nuns, it seems, were much less generously treated. Prioress Katherine Bowser of Buckland unusually received £50 (with most of her sisters receiving £4) but Prioress Cecily Verney of Cannington had £6 13s 4d and Prioress Katherine Bulle of Barrow only £5 and a gratuity of 40s. The rest of the Barrow nuns had gratuities of 20s.

The serious exception is the treatment of the community at Glastonbury. The king's commissioners reported them 'most humbly thanking the king's majesty of his great goodness most graciously showed unto them . . . as well for his gracious reward as also for their pensions'. Their pensions appear to have been small, ranging between £4 and £6 for those who still survived in 1556. What rewards they received is not known.

Regular religious community life was at an end, its former members, young and old, holy or not so holy, were scattered. Some sought the shelter of families and friends, some the life of secular priests in chapel or parish. For some the outside world had perhaps fewer attractions than they had once thought; for others, and certainly well-pensioned and amenable heads of houses, the comfort of a little manor house and even the company of former brethren may have seemed a good exchange.

Radegund Tilley, late nun of Cannington, was befriended by the Combe family of Cannington. In 1558 Bartholomew Combe left her £20 and clothing including two furred gowns. Two years later his widow Joan left her £30 and a silver goblet. Radegund had probably never been so well off in her life. Others had a different story to tell (see Appendix I).

14 Was ever the hope of restoration?

Sir John FitzJames, more sympathetic than most of his contemporaries, declared that the Glastonbury monks kept 'as good religion as any house of that order within the realm'. It was a judgement which clearly lacked enthusiasm. The question is a complex one: were there still men and women eager to continue living a life of prayer in community; were there men and women outside ready to support them adequately and to believe in their calling? The dissolution was carried out with little popular opposition, relatively little bloodshed and considerable enthusiasm. Very few continued the religious life after 1536, probably because houses still open could not afford to accept them rather than a sudden loss of vocation. After 1539 there were no alternatives at home and probably few immediately abroad.

Yet the abrupt loss of community life must have been traumatic for many who had spent their whole lives in such a socially sheltered environment and naturally enough kept in close touch with each other when their homes were closed. So when, 20 years after he was dismissed from Montacute, Robert Whitlocke the last prior, remembered four of his former brethren in his will.

Curiously it was that same community which was restored after a fashion, but our knowledge of it rests solely on the memory of an old man who gave evidence in a tithe case in court in James I's reign and recalled a time under Queen Mary when the monks had returned to Montacute. Could they have been Prior Whitlocke and his four brothers? They would have found the old buildings much changed since they came into the hands of Dr William Petre in 1539: the church had probably been demolished, the monks' graveyard was considered just a piece of land; the former prior's lodging was occupied by Petre's tenant as a farmhouse. Petre himself, Secretary of State to Henry VII, Edward VI and Queen Mary was the civil servant *par excellence* inclining to traditional religion. He alone must have been responsible for the return if the old man's memory was correct; he alone had the kind of influence necessary and held most of the land.

There were popular hopes of a revival at Glastonbury, too. Thomas Shackell of Hinton St George left £2 in his will 'to the edifying of Glastonbury abbey' and William Collyns gave money 'to the edifying of the monastery church of Glaston'. In 1557 the four former Glastonbury monks at the restored monastery at Westminster, John Phagan, John Neot, William Adelwold and William Kentwyn, petitioned the Queen for the restoration of Glastonbury. They asked for no endowment and even suggested paying rent for the buildings,

> so that without labour and husbandry we may live there, a few of us in our religious habits; and the country being so much affected to our Religion, we

61 Montacute priory gatehouse, built by Prior Thomas Chard (1514-32)

> believe we should find much help amongst them . . . whereby we would
> happily prevent the ruin of much and the repair of no little part of the whole.

It was a curious and disingenuous argument, for they went on to point out that the house had not, strictly speaking, been surrendered 'but extorted, the Abbot preposterously put to death . . .'. If this was a plea to the Queen's conscience it did not succeed; for the extorted lands, including the buildings, were firmly in the hands of rent-paying lessees, loyal supporters of the Queen's government who had paid good money for their leases and had no intention of yielding them.

Yet Queen Mary issued a charter in 1557 which restored the Carthusian house at Sheen under the leadership of Prior Maurice Chauncy, and he was joined there by John Mychell, formerly prior of Witham, and Thurstan Hyckemans, formerly of Hinton. Letters Patent were also issued in 1557 authorizing the reinstatement of the Order of St John of Jerusalem and the restoration of all land not granted away. At the end of the year James Shelley, not previously a Hospitaller, was appointed preceptor of Templecombe. Both foundations came to an end in June 1559.

From that time monastic life ceased although recusant Catholic families like the Muttleburys of Ashill, the Byfleets of Bratton Seymour and the Keyneses of Compton Pauncefoot gathered like-minded servants and neighbours around them from the 1590s. The Poyntzes of Leigh Barton in Old Cleeve, living on land once belonging to the Cistercians, set up a kind of mission centre beside their home where a succession of Benedictine monks ministered to a scattered congregation.

128

After the worst anti-Catholic legislation had been repealed groups of monks and nuns again settled in the county: Franciscan nuns at Taunton and Benedictine nuns at Cannington in 1807, Visitation nuns at Shepton Mallet in 1810, and Benedictine monks at Downside from 1814. The move to Cannington was to the very building from which nuns had been expelled in 1536. Lord and Lady Clifford, whose family had probably never abandoned the Old Faith, not only gave them a place to live; one of their daughters became a professed nun, as founders' daughters had done in the past, and from time to time their creature comforts were remembered. Family accounts include the sum of £40 to pay for a new ceiling for their chapel and treats such as peppermint drops, venison, saltfish, and *pate de Guimore* to improve an otherwise plain diet. The Cliffords also sent gifts to the sisters at Taunton.

Convents appeared in most Somerset towns by the end of the nineteenth century and most of them were rather grim and forbidding. Only the Benedictines at Downside seem to have been confident enough to move away from the camouflage of Nonconformist simplicity adopted by Catholic parish churches. They began in 1823 with a chapel attached to their original, domestic Downside House, designed in the style of contemporary Anglican 'Commissioners' churches. Only from 1872 was a new plan begun on the medieval monastic model with a large abbey church on the north side of a great cloister and now buildings of the public school to the south.

Downside has continued the great monastic tradition of learning, and among its community were Cardinal Aidan Gasquet (d.1929) and David Knowles (d.1974), in their days historians of the monastic life in England, and Aelred Watkin (d.1997), historian and titular abbot of Glastonbury. In its *Downside Review* have appeared many articles on the history of Glastonbury, and its library contains perhaps the largest collection of editions of the Rule of St Benedict, that wise guide to community living which has inspired men and women to holiness for 1,500 years.

Appendix I

Somerset Religious men and women at the dissolution

Sources

Athelney — *DKR* viii (II), 8
Barlinch — SC6/Hen VIII/7298
Barrow — *ibid.*
Bath — *L. & P. Hen. VIII*, xiv (1), 601
Bridgwater Hosp. — *DKR* viii (II), 11
Bruton — *ibid.* 12
Buckland — *ibid.* 106
Cannington — SC6/Hen VIII/7298
Cleeve — SC6/Hen VIII/7298
Hinton — *DKR* viii (II), 23
Keynsham — *ibid.* 25
Montacute — *ibid.* 32
Taunton — *ibid.* 44
Witham — *ibid.* 50
Woodspring — SC6/Hen VIII/7298

Note: Muchelney was not technically dissolved; names marked # were members of the community in 1534. *DKR* is *Report of the Deputy Keeper of the Public Records* (H.M.S.O.)

The Religious

Richard Adams, ?novice at Keynsham; alive 1556
John Aidan, monk of Glastonbury
John Aldelme, monk of Glastonbury
John Alrude, monk of Glastonbury
Aristotle Alwyn *alias* Webbe, monk of Glastonbury; married and lived in Crewkerne, died
    1577
Henry Ambrose *alias* Poyninges, monk of Athelney; alive 1556
John Ambrose, monk of Glastonbury
Nicholas Androwe, monk of Glastonbury; alive 1556
Thomas Appolyner, monk of Glastonbury
John Arimathia, monk of Glastonbury

John Arnold, canon of Keynsham; disp. to hold benefice with change of habit 1539; alive 1556

John Arthur *alias* Thorne, monk of Glastonbury, executed 1539

John Athelstan *alias* Browne, monk of Bath; disp. to hold benefice with change of habit 1539; alive 1556

Thomas Athelstan, monk of Glastonbury

William Athelwolde, monk of Glastonbury; in 1554/5 at Westminster

John Athelwyn, monk of Athelney

Richard Alvorde, canon of Bruton; alive 1556

Jane Babington, sister of Buckland; alive 1556, not 1558

Hugh Backwell or Blackwell, scholar at Oxford, canon of Bruton; alive 1556

John Bagecross or Bachecrofte, monk of Hinton; alive 1556

John Baker, monk of Cleeve

Nicholas Balland or Ballarde, monk of Hinton; monk of Sheen; 1559-78 Louvain; d.1578

John Baptyst, monk of Glastonbury

John Barwyke, prior of Barlinch

Nicholas Bathe *alias* Jobbyn, BTh, monk of Bath; disp. to hold benefice with change of habit 1539

Thomas Bathe *alias* Sexton, monk of Bath; there 1476; disp. to hold benefice with change of habit 1539

William Baylye, canon of Taunton; alive 1556

Richard Bede, monk of Glastonbury

Thomas Bede, sacrist of Keynsham; disp. to hold benefice with change of habit 1539; alive 1556

John Bekenton *alias* Romsey, monk of Bath; disp. to hold benefice with change of habit 1539; alive 1556

John Benet *alias* Parnell, monk of Bath; disp. to hold benefice with change of habit 1539; alive 1556

John Benett, monk of Cleeve; 1536-9 at Dunkeswell

John Benett, monk of Glastonbury

Geoffrey Benyng, monk of Glastonbury

John Benyng, monk of Glastonbury

Nicholas Berame, canon of Taunton; alive 1556

Richard Besyll, monk of Glastonbury

William Bewchyn, monk of Bath; disp. to hold benefice with change of habit 1539; alive 1556

John Bishop, sub-prior of Bruton; alive 1556

Alice Bisse, nun of Cannington; at Shaftesbury 1536-9

Richard Bogye, prior of Bruton

Richard Boll, prior of Athelney

Henry Bowerman, monk of Hinton; alive 1556

Joan Bowey, nun of Barrow

Katherine Bowser or Bowcher, prioress of Buckland

Thomas Brent, monk of Glastonbury

William Brente, canon of Keynsham; 1536 from Woodspring

Robert Briande, monk of Montacute

\# Stephen Bristow, monk of Muchelney 1534

William Britwolde, monk of Glastonbury

John Browne, canon of Keynsham; disp. to hold benefice with change of habit 1539; alive 1556

\# Thomas Bryge, monk of Muchelney 1534

Alexander Brystowe *alias* Bull, monk of Bath; disp. to hold benefice with change of habit 1539; alive 1556

Katherine Bull or Bowell, prioress of Barrow

William Burforde, monk of Hinton

Julian Burges, nun of Cannington

William Burges or Burgh, fraterer of Bruton; alive 1556

William Bynnesmede, canon of Taunton; alive 1556

Hugh Bytt, monk of Witham

John Carnycke, brother of St John's, Wells; alive 1556

John Castelyne, canon of Bruton; alive 1556

John Ceolffryde, monk of Glastonbury

John Chamberlayn, monk of Hinton

\# John Chedder, monk of Muchelney 1534

Richard Clerkeson, master of St John's, Wells

William Clement, monk of Bath; disp. to hold benefice with change of habit 1539; in 1554 vicar of St Mary, Stalls, Bath, aged 50 and married for four years to Elizabeth Delle, deprived; divorced

Robert Clerk, prior of Glastonbury

John Clerke, prior of Malpas, monk of Montacute; alive 1556

Thomas Cleve, monk of Glastonbury

John Clyffe, monk of Witham

Hugh Clyve, monk of Cleeve

Edmund Cokyr, monk of Glastonbury

John Cockeram, canon of Taunton; alive 1556

William Cocford, canon of Barlinch

Elizabeth Cogan, former prioress of Barrow

John Cogen, monk of Montacute

Thomas Coggyn, brother of St John's, Bridgwater

William Coke, monk of Hinton

John Colde, brother of St John's, Bridgwater

\# Richard Coscomb, prior of Muchelney 1534

\# John Combe, monk of Muchelney 1534

Isabel or Elizabeth Crewe or Grene, sister of Buckland; alive 1556, not 1558

William Crise, monk of Montacute; alive 1556

John Crybbe, monk of Montacute; in 1554 aged 63, married to Alice Slade for two years, rector of Closworth, deprived; alive 1556

William Culronde, canon of Taunton

Thomas Dale, canon of Taunton, curate of St James, Taunton

John Deryvyan *alias* Shepard, monk of Glastonbury; alive 1556

Mary Dodington, sister of Buckland

Richard Dogle, monk of Cleeve

John Dove, monk of Witham

David Dovell, monk of Cleeve

William Dovell, abbot of Cleeve; ?vicar of St Mary, Taunton, 1556-75; died 1575

Elizabeth Dune, nun of Barrow

John Dunster *alias* Hadley, BTh, chanter of Bruton; cantarist in Wells Cathedral 1543-; possibly vicar of Oborne (Dors), 1546-; rector of Kingsdon (Som), 1556-8; died by Dec. 1558

Thomas Dunston, monk of Glastonbury

William Dunston *alias* Godson, monk of Glastonbury

John Dyer, canon of Barlinch

William Dyer, monk of Montacute; alive 1556

John Dyght, canon of Taunton

John Dyte, brother of St John's, Wells; alive 1556

John Edgar *alias* Sodbury, monk of Bath; disp. to hold benefice with change of habit 1539

Roger Edgar, sub-prior of Athelney; alive 1556

Simon Edgar *alias* Enterdon, monk of Glastonbury; alive 1556

Edward Edwy *alias* Style, monk of Bath; disp. to hold benefice and change habit 1539; alive 1556

John Elphege, monk of Glastonbury

John Elye, abbot of Bruton; vicar of Pucklechurch 1541-8; d.1548

John Elys, monk of Cleeve

Alice Emerforde or Hendford, sister of Buckland

Thomas Eton, canon and cellarer of Bruton

John Exceter, monk of Glastonbury

Thomas Fletcher, monk of Hinton; alive 1556

John Fowler, canon of Keynsham

Robert Frey or Frye, monk of Hinton; alive 1556

Robert Fyssher, brother of St John's, Bridgwater; alive 1556

John Gabriell *alias* Style, monk of Bath; alive 1556

John Gaye, monk of Cleeve; 1536-9 at Dunkeswell

Thomas Genynges, monk of Athelney; alive 1556

John Gethen, monk of Cleeve

Thomas Glossyngbury, canon of Woodspring

Elizabeth Gregory, nun of Barrow

John Grene, monk of Cleeve

William Gregory, canon of Taunton

Richard Gryffythe, prior of Dunster; alive 1556

Richard Gueles *alias* Gybbys, monk of Bath; disp. to hold benefice with change habit 1539; alive 1556

Henry Gurney, monk of Hinton

Robert Gylde, monk of Glastonbury

John Gyle, canon and farmerer of Bruton

John Gylford, canon of Keynsham; disp. to hold benefice with change of habit 1539; 1554 vicar of Stratton on Fosse, aged 50

William Hadley, canon of Barlinch

Alnett Hales, monk of Witham

Robert Hamlyn, abbot of Athelney; vicar of Milton Abbot (Devon) 1554-61

John Harrold, canon of Bruton; alive 1556

John Helpes *see* Merke

Thomas Helyer, monk of Hinton; alive 1556

Laurence Herforde, monk of Montacute

William Herne or Heron, prior of Keynsham; disp. to hold benefice with change of habit 1539; alive 1556

Walter Herstone, monk of Glastonbury

Richard Herte, BD, chamberer of Bruton; alive 1556

John Heywarde, canon of Taunton; alive 1556

William Holloway *alias* Gybbys, prior of Bath; disp. to hold benefice with change of habit 1539

John Hooper, monk of Cleeve by 1519, DTh, rector of Liddington (Wilts) 1537-50+; married in Basle; chaplain to Protector Somerset; bishop of Gloucester consecrated 1551, burned 1555

Anne Hoper, nun of Barrow

Edmund Horde, prior of Hinton

George Howe, monk of Cleeve

John Humylytye *alias* Colyn, monk of Bath

Tamsin Huntyngton, sister of Buckland; alive 1558

Thomas Hurme, monk of Montacute

Thurstan Hyckemans, monk of Hinton; returned from abroad to be monk at Sheen; d.1575

Joan Hyll, sister of Buckland; alive 1558

Robert Ider *alias* Touker, monk of Glastonbury; alive 1556

Martin Indract *alias* Noble, monk of Glastonbury; alive 1556

William Joseph, monk of Glastonbury

Julian Kendall, sister of Buckland

William Kentwyn, monk of Glastonbury; 1554/5 at Westminster

Richard Kymrydge *alias* Cribbell, brother of St John's, Bridgwater; alive 1556

Hugh Lakoq, monk of Hinton

Agnes Latymer, nun of Barrow

John Laurens, monk of Athelney

John Lawson, monk of Witham

Nicholas Lychefylde, monk of Witham

Richard Lyncombe *alias* Bygg, monk of Bath; disp. to hold benefice with change of habit; alive 1556

James Marble, monk of Hinton

William Markes, brother of St John's, Wells; alive 1556

Agnes Mathew, sister of Buckland; alive 1556

Mary Mathew, sister of Buckland

Thomas Mathewe, canon of Taunton, from Barlinch 1536

Anne Maunsell or Maundefeld, sister of Buckland; alive 1556, not 1558

William Mawdesley, confessor of Buckland; alive 1556

\# Peter Meriett, monk of Muchelney 1534

John Merke or Markes *alias* Helpe, Helpes, Hilpe, Hylpe, monk of Glastonbury, born Meare; student for six years at Oxford, B.A. 1539, M.A. 1540; 1540 part of foundation of new bishopric of Westminster; fellow of Lincoln coll., Oxford, 1541-4; 1545 presented to living of Stanford Rivers, Essex; 'professing the art of physic'; rector of High Ham *c.* 1550-2; died of surfeit of fried brawn [Emden, *Biog. Reg. Univ. Oxford, 1501-40*, 310; *Proc. Som. Arch. Soc.* xl. 116]

\# Walter Mochelney, monk of Muchelney 1534

\# John Montacute, monk of Muchelney 1534

Henry Montegewe, monk of Glastonbury

John Mors, brother of St John's, Bridgwater; alive 1556

John Mychell, prior of Witham; monk at Sheen; alive 1556

John Mychelston, monk of Witham

John Mylett, monk of Witham

Robert Nelyng, monk of Hinton; alive 1556

John Neot, monk of Glastonbury; BTh; in 1554/5-9 at Westminster, where sub-prior by 1558

John Oswolde, monk of Glastonbury

John Palle or Pallye, monk of Montacute; in 1554 curate of Babcary, aged 43, married to Thomasine Bolle; mentioned in will of Robert Whitlocke, former prior of Montacute, 1560

John Pantaleon, monk of Glastonbury

Thomas Parker *alias* Alley *alias* Carter, canon of Keynsham; disp. to hold benefice with change of habit 1539; in 1554 aged 48; rector of Saltford; married Eleanor Ruffyn; deprived 1554

William Parson, canon of Taunton; alive 1556

John Partriche, canon of Keynsham; from Woodspring 1536; disp. to hold benefice with change of habit 1539 alive 1556

John Patyence *alias* Long, monk of Bath; disp. to hold benefice with change of habit 1539; alive 1556

John Pawlyn, monk of Glastonbury

John Phagan *alias* Pydesley, monk of Glastonbury; in 1554/5 at Westminster

Anne Plummer or Plumbe, sister of Buckland

Mathee Pollard, novice of Cannington

Katherine Popham, sister of Buckland; alive 1556

Thomas Powell, monk of Bath; disp. to hold benefice with change of habit 1539; alive 1556

John Pytt, sub-prior of Bath; disp. to hold benefice with change of habit 1539; alive 1556

Richard Reckeclyff, monk of Glastonbury

William Reynold, monk of Hinton

William Rogers, monk of Montacute; alive 1556

Nicholas Rowe, monk of Cleeve

Robert Savage, monk of Hinton; alive 1556

Thomas Segeforde, monk of Witham

John Selwood, monk of Glastonbury

Nicholas Serche, canon of Woodspring

Robert Skameden, monk of Hinton

John Smythe, monk of Witham

William Spencer, canon of Barlinch

John Spicer, canon of Bruton

Richard Stacye, canon of Bruton; alive 1556

John Stourton, abbot of Keynsham; disp. to hold benefice with change of habit 1539; d.1543, buried Keynsham

John Stratton, monk of Muchelney 1534

John Swanston or Swymestowe, monk of Witham; alive 1556

Margaret or Mary Sydnam, sub-prioress of Buckland

John Symes, monk of Montacute; alive 1556

John Symondes, master of St John's hosp. Bath; alive 1556

John Taunton, monk of Glastonbury

Thomas Tawnton *alias* Chiswaye, monk of Montacute; alive 1556

William Tibbett or Typpett, sub-prior of Keynsham; disp. to hold benefice with change of habit 1539; 1554 rector of Cameley, aged 41; married to Agnes Indrycke *alias* Meryett; deprived; restored to Cameley, d.1575

Radigund Tilley, nun of Cannington until 1536; at the convent of Polsloe, Devon, 1536—8; alive 1560

Roger Tormynton, prior of Woodspring; rector of Enborne (Berks) 1537-*c*.1545

Joan Towse, nun of Cannington; 1536-9 at Shaftesbury, Dorset

Margaret Tunnell, nun of Barrow

Richard Ultan, monk of Glastonbury

Nicholas Urban, monk of Glastonbury

John Veler or Fowler, canon of Keynsham; disp. to hold benefice with change of habit 1539

Cecily Verney, prioress of Cannington

John Verney, monk of Glastonbury

Patrick Vertue *alias* Archer, monk of Bath; alive 1556

John Walles, prior of Holme, monk of Montacute

Robert Walshe, master of St John's, Bridgwater

John Warren, canon of Taunton; alive 1556

John Warham, chaplain of Barrow

Robert Warrener, sub-prior of Montacute; alive 1556

\# John Water, monk of Muchelney 1534

John Webbe, sub-prior of Cleeve; 1536-9 at Dunkeswell; 1554 a JW rector of Buckland St Mary, aged 44, married to Joan Baundfelde; deprived

John Webbe, monk of Montacute; in 1554 a JW rector of Buckland St Mary, aged 44, married to Joan Baundfelde and deprived

Thomas Webber, monk of Cleeve

Nicholas Wedmore, monk of Glastonbury

John Wele, monk of Witham

Richard Welles, canon and steward of Bruton; alive 1556

Thomas Weston, monk of Glastonbury

Richard Whiting, abbot of Glastonbury, executed 1539

Robert Whitlocke *alias* Gibbes *alias* Sherborne, prior of Montacute; died 1560 at East Chinnock, buried chancel Montacute

Roger Wilffryde *alias* James, monk of Glastonbury, executed 1539

William Williams, prior of Taunton; ?rector of Silverton (Devon), 1549-52

John Woode, brother of St John's, Bridgwater; alive 1556

Richard Woodnett, monk of Witham

Richard Worcester, monk of Glastonbury

Thomas Worceter *alias* Stylbande, monk of Bath; disp. to hold benefice with change of habit, 1539; alive 1556

John Wyll, brother of St John's, Bridgwater; alive 1556

William Wylton, BCL, chaplain of Bruton

William Wynter, monk of Montacute; alive 1556

Thmas Wyther, canon of Barlinch

Henry Yne, monk of Glastonbury

Thomas Yve, abbot of Muchelney 1538

Appendix II

List of monasteries outside Somerset
which held property in the county in 1291

Some of the places have not yet been identified

Bermondsey (Surrey) £29 18s 4d
    Chilthorne Domer,
    Englishcombe,
    Kynewardeston,
    Preston,
    Stone, Yeovil
Bradenstoke (Wilts) £5 13s
    Kilmersdon,
    Limington
Breamore (Hants) £7
    Portbury,
    Stanton Drew
Bristol St Augustine's £8 9s 8d
    Kingsbury (Axbridge deanery),
    Pawlett,
    Portbury,
    Wellow
Bristol St Mark's Hospital £21
    Pawlett,
    Stockland Bristol
Bruern (Oxon) £2
    West Harptree
Canonsleigh (Devon) £4 13s 4d
    Sampford Arundel
Cirencester (Glos) £2 10s 8d
    Farleigh,
    Frome,
    Milborne Port,
    Rode,
    Woolverton

Farleigh (Wilts) 16s
    Dowlishwake,
    Timsbury
Flaxley (Glos) £11
    Blaksdon (Axbridge deanery)
Forde (Dorset) £38 16s 8d Brunkesheyne,
    Clatworthy,
    Crukehill,
    Crukesthorn,
    Winsham
Goldcliffe (Mon) £31 10s Monksilver,
    Nether Stowey,
    Preston Bowyer,
    Puriton,
    Woolavington
Hayling (Hants) £28 17s 4d Chewton Mendip,
    Ston Easton
Longleat (Wilts) £3 11s Batcombe, Laverton,
    Lullington
Merton (Surr) £19 16s 8d Midsomer Norton,
    Martock
Neath (Glam) £2 15s Exford
Ogbourne (Wilts) £26 13s 4d Old Cleeve
St Michael's Mount (Cwll) £26 13s 4d
    Martock
Shaftesbury (Dors) £33 Abbas Combe, Bath,
    Schalveston,
    Silveston
Sherborne (Dors) £5 6s Corton Denham,
    Ilchester
Stanley (Wilts) £5 7s 3d Doclonde, Estone,
    Mercombe
Studley (Warws)? £4 Trent
Tewkesbury (Glos) £6 Burnett
Wherwell (Hants) £1 6s 8d★ Bathwick
Wilmington (Sussex) £10 Norton sub Hamdon
Winchester (Hants) £4 6s 8d Bleadon
Whitland (Carms) £1 Bedminster
Wilton (Wilts) £2 8s 6d Withypool
Wormley (Herts) 7s 6d Cheddar
    ★ shared with prior of Bath

Appendix III

Ex-Religious beneficed in Somerset in 1534

Thomas Alley *alias* Carter or Barter, regular canon,
  rector of Saltford, aged 48, married to Eleanor
  Ruffyn, widow, deprived

William Bysshope, curate of Doulting, 50, regular,
  married to Alice Kymman; deprived

Thomas Froster, 'regular monk', curate of Winford,
  married to Agnes Pryer for 2 years, deprived

John Hoskyns, Franciscan friar, vicar of Charlcombe, aged
  54, married to Alice Shryve for 5 years, deprived

Henry Lewys, prebendary of Combe XV, former regular, aged
  39, married to Joan, deprived

Thomas Locke, 'regular', aged 45, vicar of Ilminster and
  rector of Hatch Beauchamp, married to Joan Hawker,
  deprived [probably Thomas Bryge, monk of Muchelney in
  1534]

Thomas Male, 'regular monk', curate of South Petherton,
  aged 50, married to Joan Lacye, deprived

Thomas Mychell, 'regular', divorced from Emma Corden

Henry Nele, Carmelite friar, curate of St Catherine, aged
  61, married to Elizabeth Payne, widow, for 4 years,
  deprived

Robert Pytman, monk of Sherborne, vicar of Woolavington,
  married to Joan; deprived

Peter Smyth 'sometime religious' married and living in
  Bridgwater 1555

Bartholomew Storre, monk of Sherborne; aged 40, married
  to Christian Lane for 2 years, rector of Thorn
  Coffin, deprived

John Trevylian, regular in minor orders, married to Alice
  Palmer

James Wickham, regular canon, rector of Chewstoke, aged
  44, married to Elizabeth Myller for 2 years, deprived

John ?, aged 28 regular in minor orders, married to Edith
  Rayneld for 4 years

Appendix IV
Gazeteer of Somerset religious houses

[Abbreviations: BL British Library; *DR Downside Review*; PRO Public Record Office; *Proc. Som. Arch. Soc. Proceedings Somerset Archaeological Society*; RO Record Office; *SDNQ Somerset and Dorset Notes and Queries*; SRS Somerset Record Society; *VCH Victoria County History*]

ATHELNEY
Benedictine abbey of St Saviour, St Peter, St Paul and Athelwine, founded *c.*888 by King Alfred. 9 monks (plus two absent and apostate) in 1458, 11 in 1485, 13 in 1534, 9 in 1539. Dissolved 1539. Site of abbey church marked by 1801 monument.
Sources: *VCH Somerset*, ii. 99-103; Dunning, 'The Abbey of the Princes: Athelney Abbey, Somerset'; *Proc. Som. Arch. Soc.* xliii. 94-165; SRS xiv, passim.; Devon R.O. 123M/01 (Ilton).

BARLINCH
Priory of Augustinian canons dedicated to St Nicholas and founded 1174 x 1191, possibly by William de Say. 7 canons in 1456, 3 in 1488, 4 in 1492, 9 in 1524, 7 in 1536. Dissolved 1536. Parts of priory incorporated in farm buildings. NE window in Huish Champflower church said to be from priory.
Sources: *VCH Somerset*, ii. 132-4; PRO SC 6/Hen. VIII/7298 (1536); *Proc. Som. Arch. Soc.* liv. 79-106; *ibid.* cxxviii (1984), 55-63; *ibid.* cxxxiv (1990), 183-5; *Chapters of Augustinian Canons* (Cant. & York Soc.), 184.

BARROW GURNEY (MINCHIN BARROW)
Priory of Benedictine nuns dedicated to the Blessed Virgin and St Edwin or St Edward, king and martyr, probably by Hawise de Gurney, before *c.*1201. 8 nuns 1536. Dissolved 1536.
Sources: PRO SC 6/Hen. VIII/7298 (1536); *V.C.H. Somerset*, ii. 107-9; *Proc. Som. Arch. Soc.* xii. 46-147.

BATH
Benedictine abbey of St Peter and St Paul. Refounded as abbey *c.*963; cathedral priory from 1090. 41 monks in 1206, 17 in 1377, 22 in 1476, 22 in 1525, 16 in 1534. Dissolved 1539.
Sources: Wells Cathedral Libr. charter 41 (1180); *ibid.* MS V4/08 (precedent bk.); SRS vii. passim; lvi. 83-5; J. Maclean, *History of Trigg Minor* i. 638n. *Proc. Som. Arch. Soc.* cxxxvii 75--log

BATH

Hospital of St John the Baptist, founded *c*.1180 by Bishop Reginald FitzJocelin for the poor of the city and associated with the baths. 1377 prior and 4 brothers. Hospital still functioning.
Source: Manco, *Spirit of Care*, 15-20, 26-38.

BATH

Hospital of St Mary Magdalen, Holloway, for lepers. First mentioned 1212; master and brothers mentioned 1256; sisters there *c*.1270 were probably nurses.
Source: Manco, *Spirit of Care*, 20-6.

BRIDGWATER

Hospital founded by William Brewer. 12 canons in 1534, 8 in 1539. Dissolved 1539.
Sources: SRS lv. 45; *V.C.H. Somerset*, ii. 154—6; vi. 202-3.

BRIDGWATER

Franciscan Friary founded *c*.1230 with help of William Brewer. 7 in 1538. Dissolved 1538.
Sources: VCH Somerset, ii. 151-2; vi. 203; Leland, *Itinerary*, i, 163; SRS xxxi. 170.

BRUTON

Augustinian priory, from 1511 abbey, founded in 1142 by William de Mohun, earl of Somerset, probably in succession to a minster founded by St Aldhelm in the seventh century. 15 canons in 1377, 16 in 1430, 18 in 1534, 15 in 1539. Dissolved 1539. Site incorporated in mansion of Berkeley family which was demolished by the Hoares in the late eighteenth century. Part of precinct wall survives W of parish church in street called Plox. The so-called abbey dovecote was not originally a dovecote and was built long after the abbey had been dissolved.
Sources: VCH Somerset, ii. 134-8; vii. 25; SRS viii, passim; *Cal. Inq. p.m.* ii, p. 21; Maxwell-Lyte, *History of Dunster*, i. 114; *Sarum Charters and Docs.* (Rolls Series), 225-6; SRO DD/HI box 5; *ibid.* DD/PE 7; *ibid.* DD/SAS PF 56; Glos. R.O. D547a/M6; PRO SC6/Hen VIII/3137.

BRUTON

Hospital of St Catherine, Lusty, founded by 1291; in later fourteenth century took lepers and other sick; became almshouse.
Source: VCH Somerset, vii. 42.

BUCKLAND (MINCHIN BUCKLAND)

Began as priory of Augustinian canons *c*.1166 on foundation of William de Erlegh; before *c*.1180/86 canons replaced by sisters of order of Knights Hospitaller. 14 sisters in 1539. Dissolved 1539. Site at east end of Durston village, now occupied by Buckland Farm.
Sources: VCH Somerset, ii. 148-50; vi. 259; *Cal. Pat.* 1307-13, 385; *L & P Hen. VIII*, xiv(1) p106 (pension list); E. Power, *Med. Eng. Nunneries*, 37-8; *Proc. Som. Arch. Soc.* x. 1-112.

BURTLE

Priory of the Holy Trinity, the Blessed Virgin Mary and St Stephen at Sprawlesmead; dependent on Glastonbury after 1270 although Augustinian. Called *ecclesia collegiata* in 1335. Sometimes named Brademers by the Augustinians. 2 in 1377.
Sources: *VCH Somerset*, ii. 139; SRS lix, p. 11; *Chapters of Augustinian Canons* (Cant. & York Soc.).

CANNINGTON

Benedictine nunnery of St Mary founded between *c*.1129 and *c*.1153 probably by Robert de Curci. 11 nuns in 1317, 6 in 1536. Dissolved in 1536. Nunnery converted to mansion at Dissolution but became a nunnery again 1807-*c*.1835, 1863-7; layout of original building still retained in house now occupied by Cannington College.
Sources: SC 6/Hen.VIII/7298 (1536); Ugbrooke, Clifford MSS. accts. 1795-1829); *Proc. Som. Arch. Soc.* xi. 1-121; *VCH Somerset*, ii. 109-11; vi. 77.

CLEEVE

Cistercian abbey founded 1198 by William de Roumare. In 1297, 26 monks, 28 thereafter, 10 in 1525, 15 in 1536. Dissolved 1536. Site in care of English Heritage includes extensive cloistral buildings and foundations of abbey church.
Sources: PRO E 315/91; *ibid.* SC 6/Hen.VIII/7298 (1536); Dunning, 'The Last Days of Cleeve Abbey'; *VCH Somerset*, ii. 115-18; *ibid.* v. 42, 44; *Proc. Som. Arch. Soc.* lii. 1-41; *H.M.C. Wells MSS.* ii. 577-8.

DUNSTER

Benedictine priory, founded in 1090 as a cell of Bath by William de Mohun and his wife. One monk 1539. Site adjacent to parish church, part of which was used by monks; dovecote.
Sources: *VCH Somerset*, ii. 81-2; H.C. Maxwell-Lyte, *History of Dunster*, ii, chapter xii.

GLASTONBURY

Benedictine abbey of St Mary. 72 *c*.1160, 49 in 1199, 81 in 1322, 54 in 1368, 53 in 1370-1, 45 in 1377, 52 in 1408, 57 in 1446-7, 53 in 1456, 47 in 1524, 52 in 1534, 54 in 1538-9. Dissolved 1539 when abbot and two monks executed. Site in centre of town comprising Lady Chapel and undercroft, part of nave, crossing and choir; kitchen and part of hall of abbot's lodgings; chapel of former almshouses; Tor with tower of chapel of St Michael.
Sources: SRO D/D/B misc 1; B.L. Egerton MSS. 3034, 3134 (Abbot Bere's Terrier); Longleat MS. 39A; Wells Cath. Libr. A.H. 12 (almonry school), 103 (seal, 1398); *DR* ix. 201; xi. 150-1; lxvii. 76-86, 437-50; xcv. 306—15; SRS v, xxvi, xxxix, lix, lxiii-iv; Dunning, 'Revival at Glastonbury 1530-9; *Proc. Som. Arch. Soc.* civ. 97-101; *ibid.* cvii. 79-92; cviii. 113-31; *SDNQ* xxviii. 86-90, 129-33, 159-61, 181-4; *VCH Somerset*, ii. 82-99; *Cal. Papal Letters* xi. 98; *L & P Hen. VIII.* vii, p. 411; *Registrum Epistolarum Fr. Johannis Peckham* (Rolls Series), 259-65.

HINTON

Carthusian priory of St Mary the Virgin, St John the Baptist and All Saints, founded 1227-32 by Ela, Countess of Salisbury. 17 in 1534, 17 in 1539. Dissolved 1539. Remains of chapter house with library over, refectory undercroft, sacristy and guesthouse; church and cloister excavated in 1950s.

Sources: *SDNQ* viii. 216-17, 294-7; Thompson, *Somerset Carthusians*; *VCH Somerset*, ii. 118-23; *Proc. Som. Arch. Soc.* xcvi. 160-5; *ibid.* ciii. 76-80; Dunning, 'West-Country Carthusians'.

ILCHESTER

Dominican Friary, founded by 1263. Seven in 1538. Dissolved 1538.
Source: *VCH Somerset*, ii. 150-1; *ibid.* iii. 182.

ILCHESTER

Hospital for poor pilgrims and travellers, founded by 1220; priory under prioress, called Blanchesale or Whitehall, possibly Augustinian, by 1281. Prioress and 2 in 1334. Prioress and 1 in 1423. Converted to free chapel by 1463.
Source: *VCH Somerset*, iii. 196-8.

KEYNSHAM

Augustinian abbey of St Mary of Victorine family, founded *c.*1172 by William, earl of Gloucester, in memory of his son Robert. 18 canons in 1377, 14 in 1526, 16 in 1534, 11 (12) in 1539. Dissolved 1539. Site of abbey church largely excavated in advance of bypass in 1960s.
Sources: PRO E 315/102; Vincent, 'Early Years of Keynsham Abbey'; *VCH Somerset*, ii. 129-32; *Proc. Som. Arch. Soc.* liii. 15-63.

MONTACUTE

Cluniac priory of St Peter and St Paul founded *c.*1107 by William, count of Mortain. 25 monks in 1262, 20 in 1276, 28 in 1279, 24 *c.*1298, 26
in 1304, 10 in 1377, 24 in 1450, 14 in 1539 (3 others at Malpas, 2 at Holme). Dissolved 1539; refounded for a short time under Queen Mary. Gatehouse and prior's lodging a private house south-west of the parish church.
Sources: *Visitations of English Cluniac Foundations*, ed. G.F. Duckett, 12, 17, 38; PRO SC 11/798 (survey 1304); Devon RO 123M/O2 (account 1537-8); *VCH Somerset*, ii. 111-15; *Cal. Pat.* 1452-61, 470.

MUCHELNEY

Benedictine abbey of St Peter and St Paul founded probably eighth century by King Ine (d.726), refounded *c.*950. 17 monks in 1381, 13 in 1463, 15 in 1489, 11 in 1534, 11 in 1538 when surrendered. Foundations of church, part of cloister, abbot's lodging and associated buildings, reredorter in care of English Heritage. Almonry barn under separate ownership.
Sources: PRO SC 12/14/38 (fees *c.*1535); ibid. E 134/7 James I/Mich. 16 (evidence of aged witness); stock account in possession of G. Stevens Cox, Guernsey; SRO DD/AB 10-12

(rentals 1407-44); SRS xiv, xlii; *VCH Somerset*, ii. 103-7; *ibid.* iii. 40, 42; *Proc. Som. Arch. Soc.* viii. 76-132.

STAVORDALE

Augustinian priory of St James of the Victorine congregation, founded by 1243. Incorporated in Taunton priory 1533. Perhaps 8 canons 1400, 6 in 1533. Probably conventual life ceased thereafter.
Sources: *VCH Somerset*, ii. 139-41; *Proc. Som. Arch. Soc. l. 94-103.*

TAUNTON

Augustinian priory of St Peter and St Paul founded 1120-25 by William Giffard, bishop of Winchester, probably in succession to an eighth-century minster. New site outside town *c.*1158 by Henry of Blois, bishop of Winchester. 26 canons in 1339, 15 in 1377, 15 in 1534, 12 in 1539. Dissolved 1539. Part of entrance to outer court familiarly known as Priory Barn and converted to a cricket museum. Site of part of priory graveyard including bell-pit excavated.
Sources: SRO DD/SP 408 (1415-20); *VCH Somerset*, ii. 141-4; *Proc. Som. Arch. Soc.* ix. 1-127; *Archaeology of Taunton*, ed. P. Leach, 104-6, 111-24.

TAUNTON

A chapel of St Margaret *infirmorum* was in existence by 1180 which in 1236 was said in a royal writ (but in no other source) to have been run by a master and brethren for lepers. In 1307 a canon from Taunton priory was master and the clientele were poor and sick. The foundation later became an almshouse. Buildings, much altered and damaged, stand east of the town centre, locally in West Monkton parish.
Sources: *Proc. Som. Arch. Soc.* xviii. 100-35; *ibid.* cv. 52-60.

TEMPLE COMBE

House of Knights Templar founded by Serlo FitzOdo *c.*1185; suppressed with the Order 1312-13 and house became a preceptory of Knights Hospitaller. 6 brothers in 1338. Dissolved 1540.
Sources: *VCH Somerset*, ii. 146-7; *ibid.* vii. 78-9; King, *Six Documents . . . Grand Priories.*

WELLS

Hospital of St John the Baptist, founded 1212 x 1235. 4 brothers in 1539. Dissolved 1539. Most buildings removed in 1858, having most recently been partly a school, partly a shop. A house known as The Priory of St John on an adjoining site not part of the foundation.
Sources: PRO E 315/102 (debt to Brampson); *VCH Somerset*, ii. 158-60; T. Serel, *Hist. Notes. St Cuthbert, Wells*, 122-131; SDNQ xxxi. 32-3.

WITHAM

Carthusian priory of St Mary the Virgin, St John Baptist and All Saints, founded from La Grande Chartreuse 1178 x 81 by Henry II. 14 monks in 1539. Dissolved 1539. Site of cloister in pasture land with fishponds below; church of lay brothers the present parish church of Witham Friary. Nearby dovecote later converted to parish library.

Sources: Thompson, *Somerset Carthusians*; *VCH Somerset*, ii. 123-8; Dunning, 'West-Country Carthusians'; *SDNQ* viii. 217; Wells Cath. MS. ADD/9 (foundation charter); P.R.O. C 66/744 (sale 1540); *Proc. Som. Arch. Soc.* lxiv. 1-28. cxxxiv.141-82.

WOODSPRING

Priory of Augustinian canons dedicated to the Holy Trinity, St Mary the Virgin and St Thomas of Canterbury, founded by William de Courtenay originally (*c*.1210) at a place called Dodlinch near North Curry and here before 1226. A member of Victorine Order with Keynsham and Stavordale. 9 canons in 1377, 8 in 1534, 5 in 1536. Dissolved 1536. Owned by Landmark Trust; priory church converted to dwellings at Dissolution; barn still in agricultural use.

Sources: PRO SC 6/Hen.VIII/7298; Tomalin, *Woodspring Priory*; *VCH Somerset*, ii. 144-6; *Proc. Som. Arch. Soc.* li. 10-30.

YENSTON

Estate granted by Hugh, earl of Chester ?1085 to St Sever (Calvados); priory apparently established by 1225; last mentioned 1347. Old stones of the priory sold 1450, some remaining 1454. New house on site by 1516.

Sources: Eton College Records 60/LB/1, 61/RR/A/61; *Cal. Close Rolls* 1346-9, 288; SRS vi. 16; xi, p. 92; *VCH Somerset*, vii. 113-14.

Bibliography

[Sources for individual houses are to be found in the Gazetteer, Appendix IV]

Manuscript sources

Devon Record Office, Exeter: Register of Bishop Richard Fox
Public Record Office, Kew: E 315/91, 102: monastic agreements. E 315/232-3, 244-5: patents for pensions.
Somerset Record Office, Taunton: D/D/B reg 7-12: registers of Bishops Stillington, Fox, King, Hadrian, Wolsey and Clerk (unprinted ordination lists). D/D/Vc 66: list of religious and others deprived for marriage, 1554.
Wiltshire and Swindon Record Office, Trowbridge: Register of Bishop William Aiscough, 1438-50.

Printed Sources

(Calendar of) Close Rolls (H.M.S.O.), 1227-1509.
Calendar of Papal Registers: Letters (H.M.S.O.) 1198-1492.
Calendar of Papal Registers: Letters (Irish MSS. Commission) 1484-1513.
Calendar of Papal Registers: Petitions (H.M.S.O.), 1342-1419.
(Calendar of) Patent Rolls (H.M.S.O.), 1216-1509.
Two Cartularies of Bath Priory, ed. W. Hunt (Somerset Record Soc. vii. 1893).
Two Cartularies of . . . Bruton and . . . Montacute (Somerset Record Soc. viii, 1894).
Cartularies of Muchelney and Athelney Abbeys, ed. E.H. Bates (Somerset Record Soc. xiv. 1899).
Cartulary of Buckland Priory, ed. F.W. Weaver (Somerset Record Soc. xxv. 1909).
Chapters of the Augustinian Canons, ed. H.E. Salter (Canterbury and York Soc. 1922).
Great Chartulary of Glastonbury, ed. A. Watkin (Somerset Record Soc. lix, lxiii-iv. 1947-56).
Christ Church, Canterbury, ed. W. G. Searle (Cambridge Antiquarian Soc. Octavo Publications 34 (1902).
The Chronicle of John of Glastonbury, ed. J.P. Carley (1985).
'The Chronicle of John Somer, OFM', ed. J. Catto and L. Mooney, *Camden Miscellany*, xxxiv (1997).
Custumaria of Glastonbury Abbey, ed. C.J. Elton (Somerset Record Soc. v. 1891).
Dean Cosyn and Wells Cathedral Miscellanea, ed. A. Watkin (Somerset Record Soc. lvi. 1941).
Documents Illustrating the Activities of the General and Provincial Chapters of the English Black Monks, 1215-40, ed. W.A. Pantin (Camden Soc. 3 vols. 1931-7).
A Feodary of Glastonbury Abbey, ed. F.W. Weaver (Somerset Record Soc. xxvi. 1910).
'Glastonbury Abbey in 1322', ed. T.F. Palmer in *Collectanea i* (Somerset Record Soc. xxxix. 1924).
Die Heiligen Englands, ed. F. Liebermann (1889).
The Itinerary of John Leland, ed. L. Toulmin Smith (5 vols. 1907 and 1964).
Letters from the English Abbots to the Chapter at Citeaux, 1442-1521, ed. C.H. Talbot (Camden Soc. 4th series, iv, 1967).
Letters and Papers of Henry VIII (H.M.S.O.) 1509-40.
The Maire of Bristowe is Kalendar, Robert Ricart, ed. L.T. Smith (Camden Soc. 1872).
Manuscripts of the Dean and Chapter of Wells (Historical MSS. Commission 1907, 1914).
Memorials of Henry VII, ed. J. Gairdner (Rolls Series 1864).
Muchelney Memoranda, ed. B. Schofield (Somerset Record Soc. xlii. 1927).
Register of Bishop Bekynton, ed. H.C. Maxwell-Lyte and M.C.B. Dawes (Somerset Record Soc. xlix, l. 1934-5).
Register of Bishop Bubwith, ed. T.S. Holmes (Somerset Record Soc. xxix-xxx. 1913-14).

Register of Bishops, 1518-59, ed. H.C. Maxwell-Lyte (Somerset Record Soc. lv. 1940).
Register of John Drokensford, ed. E. Hobhouse (Somerset Record Soc. i. 1887).
Registers of Bishops Giffard and Bowet, ed. T.S. Holmes (Somerset Record Soc. xiii. 1899).
Registers of Oliver King and Hadrian de Castello, ed. H.C. Maxwell-Lyte (Somerset Record Soc. liv. 1939).
Register of Ralph of Shrewsbury, ed. T.S. Holmes (Somerset Record Soc. ix, x. 1895-6).
Register of Bishop Stafford, ed. T.S. Holmes (Somerset Record Soc. xxxi, xxxii. 1915-16).
Register of Edmund Stafford, ed. F.C. Hingeston-Randolph (1886).
Registers of Bishop Stillington and Bishop Fox, ed. H.C. Maxwell-Lyte (Somerset Record Soc. lii. 1937).
Sarum Charters and Documents, ed. W.R. Jones and W.D. Macray (Rolls Series 1891).
Six Documents relating to Queen Mary's Restoration of the Grand Priories of England and Ireland, ed. E.J. King (1935).
Somerset Wills, XIVth and XVth Centuries, ed. F.W. Weaver (Somerset Record Soc. xvi. 1901).
Somerset Wills, 1501-30, ed. F.W. Weaver (Somerset Record Soc. xix. 1903).
Somerset Wills, 1531-58, ed. F.W. Weaver (Somerset Record Soc. xxi. 1905).
Star Chamber Proceedings, Henry VII and Henry VIII, ed. G. Bradford (Somerset Record Soc. xxvii. 1911).
Stogursey Chartulary, ed. T.D. Tremlett (Somerset Record Soc. lxi. 1949).
Taxatio Ecclesiastica Angliae et Walliae Auctoritate P. Nicholai IV (Record Commission 1802).
Valor Ecclesiasticus (Record Commission 1810).
'Visitation of Religious Houses and Hospitals, 1526', ed. T.F. Palmer, *Collectanea* i (Somerset Record Soc. 1924).
Thomas Walsingham, *Historia Anglicana* iii, ed. H.T. Riley (Rolls Series 1864).
William Worcestre, Itineraries, ed. J.H. Harvey (1969).

Secondary works

W.A.J. Archbold, *The Somerset Religious Houses* (1892).
M. Aston, *Monasteries in the Landscape* (2000).
J.H. Bettey, *Suppression of the Monasteries in the West Country* (1989).
N. Brooks, *The Early History of the Church of Canterbury* (1984).
I. Burrow, 'Mynchin Buckland Priory — topographical notes', *Somerset Archaeology and Natural History*, cxxix (1985), 110-13.
I. Burrow and C.B. Burrow, 'Witham Priory: the First English Carthusian Monastery', *Somerset Archaeology and Natural History*, cxxxiv (1990), 141-82.
J.P. Carley, 'Sixty-Three Monks who entered Glastonbury Abbey', *Downside Review* xcv (1977), 306-15.
J.P. Carley, 'John Leland at Somerset Libraries', *Somerset Archaeology and Natural History* cxxix (1985), 141-54.
J.P. Carley, 'John Leland and the Contents of English Pre-Dissolution Libraries: Glastonbury Abbey', *Scriptorium* xl (1986), 1, 107-20.
J.P. Carley, *Glastonbury Abbey* (1988).
J.P. Carley, 'More pre-Conquest manuscripts from Glastonbury Abbey', *Anglo-Saxon England*, 23 (1995), pp265-81.
C.M. Church, *Chapters in the Early History of the Church of Wells* (1894).
N. Coldstream and P. Draper (eds.), *Medieval Art and Architecture at Wells and Glastonbury* (British Archaeological Association, 1981).
R.A. Croft *et al.*, note on Athelney survey in 'Somerset Archaeology 1993' in *Somerset Archaeology and Natural History* cxxxvii (1993), 142-3.
Corpus of British Medieval Library Catalogues 4, eds. R. Sharpe, J.P. Carley, R.M. Thomson and A.G. Watson (British Library and British Academy 1996).
D. Dales, *Dunstan: Saint and Statesman* (1988).
G.F. Duckett, *Visitations and Chapters of the Order of Cluny* (1893).
R. Dunning, 'Revival at Glastonbury 1530-9', *Renaissance and Renewal in Christian History* (Studies in Church History 14) ed. D. Baker (1977).
R. Dunning, 'The Last Days of Cleeve Abbey', *The Church in Pre-Reformation Society*, ed. C. Barron and C. Harper-Bill (1985).

R. Dunning, 'The Abbey of the Princes: Athelney Abbey, Somerset', *Kings and Nobles in the Later Middle Ages*, edd. R.A. Griffiths and J. Sherborne (1986).

R. Dunning, *Arthur: the King in the West* (1988).

R. Dunning, 'The West-Country Carthusians', *Religious Belief and Ecclesiastical Careers in Late Medieval England*, ed. C. Harper-Bill (1991).

F.A. Gasquet, 'List of Glastonbury Monks and Others of their Household in AD 1377', *Downside Review* xi (1892), 150-1.

T. Hugo, *Medieval Nunneries* (1867)

A.F. Judd, *The Life of Thomas Bekynton* (1961).

I.J.E. Keil, 'The Garden at Glastonbury Abbey: 1333-4', *P.S.A.S.* civ (1959-60), 96-101.

I.J.E. Keil, 'The Chamberer of Glastonbury Abbey in the Fourteenth Century', *ibid.* cvii (1962-3), 79-92.

I.J.E. Keil, 'Corrodies of Glastonbury Abbey in the Later Middle Ages', *ibid.* cviii (1963-4), 113-31.

I.J.E. Keil, 'Profiles of some abbots of Glastonbury', *Downside Review*, lxxxi (1963), 355-70.

I.J.E. Keil, 'The Granger of Glastonbury Abbey, 1361-2', *S.D.N.Q.* xxviii (1964), 86-90.

I.J.E. Keil, 'The Archdeaconry of Glastonbury in the Later Middle Ages', *ibid.* 129-33.

I.J.E. Keil, 'Some Taxation Assessments of the Income of Glastonbury Abbey', *ibid.* 159-61.

I.J.E. Keil, 'Mills on the Estates of Glastonbury Abbey in the Later Middle Ages', *ibid.* 181-4.

N.R. Ker (ed.), *Medieval Libraries of Great Britain* (2nd edn. 1964).

D. Knowles, *The Monastic Order in England* (1950).

D. Knowles, *The Religious Orders in England* (3 vols. 1956-7, 1959).

D. Knowles, *The Episcopal Colleagues of Archbishop Thomas Becket* (1951).

J. Manco, 'The Buildings of Bath Priory', *Proc. Som. Arch. Soc.* cxxxvii (1993), 75-109.

J. Manco, *The Spirit of Care: the eight-hundred-year story of St John's Hospital, Bath* (1998).

H.C. Maxwell-Lyte, *A History of Dunster* (2 vols. 1909).

H. Mayr-Harting (ed.), *Saint Hugh of Lincoln* (1987).

J.R.H. Moorman, 'The Foreign Elements among the English Franciscans', *English Historical Review*, lxii (1947), 298.

W.F. [Emons-] Nijenhuis, *The Vision of Edmund Leversedge* (Doctoral thesis, Nijmegen, 1990).

G. Oliver, *Monasticon Diocesis Exoniensis* (1846).

N. Orme, *Education in the West of England 1066-1548* (1976).

N. Orme, 'A School Note-Book from Barlinch Priory', *Proc. Som. Arch. Soc.* CXXVIII (1984), 55-63.

N. Orme, 'More Pages from a Barlinch Schoolbook', *ibid.* cxxxiv. 183-5.

N. Orme and M. Webster, *The English Hospital* (1995)

E. Power, *Medieval English Nunneries* (1922).

J. Armitage Robinson, 'The Foundation Charter of Witham Charterhouse', *Proceedings of the Somerset Archaeological and Natural History Society* lxiv (1918), 1-28.

J. Sayers, 'Monastic Archdeacons' in *Church and Government in the Middle Ages*, ed. C.N.L. Brooke, D.E. Luscombe, G.H. Martin, and D.M. Owen (1976), 177-203.

T. Serel, *Historical Notes on the Church of St. Cuthbert, Wells* (1875).

D. Sherlock, *Signs for Silence* (1992).

P. Sims-Williams, 'Continental influence at Bath monastery in the seventh century', *Anglo-Saxon England* 4 (1975), 1-10.

T.B. Snow, 'Glastonbury', *Downside Review* ix (1890), 201.

N.E. Stacey, 'The Estates of Glastonbury Abbey' (Oxford D. Phil. thesis 1971).

E.M. Thompson, *The Somerset Carthusians* (1895).

S. Thompson, *Women Religious* (1991).

D.J. Tomalin, *Woodspring Priory* (1974).

N. Vincent, 'The Early Years of Keynsham Abbey', *Trans. Bristol and Gloucestershire Arch. Soc.* cxi (1993), 95-113.

A. Watkin, 'Last Glimpses of Glastonbury', *Downside Review* 67, no. 207 (1948), 76-86.

A. Watkin, 'Glastonbury, 1538-9, as shown by its Account Rolls', *Downside Review* 67, no. 210 (1949), 437-50.

A.G. Watson, *Medieval Libraries of Great Britain, Supplement* (1987).

E.H.D. Williams *et al*, 'The George Inn, Norton St Philip, Somerset', *Archaeological Journal* 144 (1987), 317-27.

T.W. Williams, *Somerset Medieval Libraries* (1897).

M. Williams, *The Draining of the Somerset Levels* (1970).

Index

Abbreviations: abb - abbey, abbot; archd - archdeacon; bp - bishop; br - brother; c - canon; diss - dissolved; m - monk; pr - prior; prss - prioress; pry - priory; sis - sister; suff – suffragan. All places are in Somerset unless otherwise stated.